Religions and Beliefs

Series Editor: Ina Taylor

Buddhism

Gary Beesley

Nelson Thornes

Published in 2006 by:
Nelson Thornes Ltd
Delta Place
27 Bath Road
CHELTENHAM
GL53 7TH
United Kingdom

11 / 10 9 8 7 6 5 4 3

A catalogue record for this book is available from the British Library

ISBN 978 0 7487 9674 8

Edited by Judi Hunter
Picture research by Sue Sharp
Illustrations by Angela Lumley and Harry Venning
Page make-up by eMC Design

Printed by Multivista Global Ltd

Acknowledgements

With thanks to the following for permission to reproduce photographs and other copyright material in this book:

Cover photo: Thinkstock/ Alamy

Alamy/ Tibor Bognor: 61B; Alamy/ David Hamilton: 8A; Alamy/ Imagestate/ Pictor International: 34A (top); Alamy/ Phototake Inc: 12A (centre); Alamy/ Pictures Colour Library: 25 (background); Alamy/ Dan White: 35C; The Amaravati Sangha: 23C; Andy Weber Studios: 5, 15B, 29C, 42; Arkreligion.com/ Tibor Bognor: 44A; Arkreligion.com/ Esther James: 57C; Art Directors & Trip Photolibrary: 34A (bottom); Gary Beesley: 36 (all); Bodhikusuma Buddhist & Meditation Centre: 54B; Bridgeman Art Library/ Adoration of the Buddha, Indian School, (20th century)/ Private Collection, Ann & Bury Peerless Picture Library: 18A; Bridgeman Art Library/ Death and the Pedlar, from 'The Dance of Death', engraved by Hans Luutzelburger, c.1538 (woodcut) (b/w photo), Holbein, Hans the Younger (1497/8–1543) (after)/ Private Collection: 25 (inset); Bridgeman Art Library/ Sir Isaac Newton, Anonymous/ Petworth House, West Sussex, UK: 13; Corbis/ Joe McDonald: 49C (top); Corbis/ Kevin R Morris: 53B; Corbis/ Leonard de Selva: 30A (left); Corbis/ Larry Williams: 39C (left); Corbis/ Alison Wright: 21E; Corbis/ M Taner/ Zefa: 23B; Corel 315 (NT): 23A; Empics/ AP/ Inge Gjellesvik: 59C; Getty Images: 39C (right); Getty Images/ Tim Graham Picture Library: 41B; Holt Studios: 48B; Illustrated London News V2 (NT): 21 (bottom right); The ImiTate© Gallery: 46B; Tanya Jäger: 32A, 33B and C; John Birdsall Photography: 9B; Ajahn Khemadhammo: 61A & B; Magnum

Photos/ Marc Riboud: 56B; Michelangelo/ Corel 301 (NT): 20A; Museum of Ethnography, Stockholm, Sweden: 19B; Sheena Napier: 40A; Nature Picture Library/ Thoswan Devakul: 43A (right); Panos Pictures: 29D (bottom right); Kevin Peterson/ Photodisc 33 (NT): 12 (top left, bottom left and right), 37E (both), 39C (middle); Photodisc 29 (NT): 22–23 (background); Photodisc 34 (NT): 20–21 (background); Photofusion: 29D (top), 31B; Popperfoto: 58A (both); Report Digital/ Phillip Wolmuth: 10A; Rex Features: 38A (left), 45D; Rex Features/ Laski Diffision: 49D; Rex Features/ Everett Collection: 38A (top right); Rex Features/ Alex Segre: 48A; Rex Features/ Sipa Press: 38A (bottom right); Rex Features/ Phil Yeomans: 38A (middle); Ronald Grant Archive/ Mandalay Entertainment/ Tristar Pictures: 59B; Ronald Grant Archive/ Warner Brothers: 7B; RSPCA Photo Library: 45E; Sally & Richard Greenhill: 12 (top right), 30A (right); Science Photo Library: 49C (bottom); Still Pictures/ Mark Edwards: 43; Still Pictures/ Shezad Noorani: 45C; Still Pictures: 54A.

Extract from speech made by HRH Prince Charles at the London Buddhist Vihara (page 40) reproduced from www.princeofwales.gov.uk.

The author also wishes to thank David Armstrong, Diana Bahamon, Paul Haddon, Tanja Jäger and Franz Novotny.

Every effort has been made to contact copyright holders. The publishers apologise to anyone whose rights have been inadvertently overlooked, and will be happy to rectify any errors or omissions.

Contents

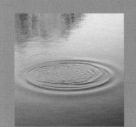
 # Fast facts about Buddhism

Q When did Buddhism begin?

2,500 years ago – Buddhism is the third oldest of the six major world religions. It began in what is now India. It was founded by Siddhartha Gotama, who took the title the Buddha, meaning 'The Enlightened One'.

Q What is Buddhism?

Buddhists do not believe in a God. Buddhism teaches that people can come to understand the real meaning of existence for themselves.

Q Types of Buddhism

Buddhists are followers of two main traditions: the Theravada or 'Tradition of the Elders', and the Mahayana or 'Great Vehicle'. About 105 million Buddhists are Theravadins, while there are somewhere in the region of 390 million Mahayanists.

While the main goal for a Theravada Buddhist is to escape the cycle of birth and death by achieving personal liberation or 'nirvana', the main goal of Mahayana Buddhists is to achieve 'enlightenment' in order to free all beings from suffering.

This book covers the teachings contained in each of these traditions. However, it contains more information on Mahayana Buddhism than is often found in textbooks. This should give students the opportunity to learn about the diversity of beliefs within the Buddhist faith, rather than developing an understanding of only one tradition within it.

Q How many Buddhists are there?

Around 7% of the world's population or 495 million people are Buddhists in the world today. 45,000 of them live and practise in the UK. This makes Buddhism the world's fourth largest religion and the UK's sixth.

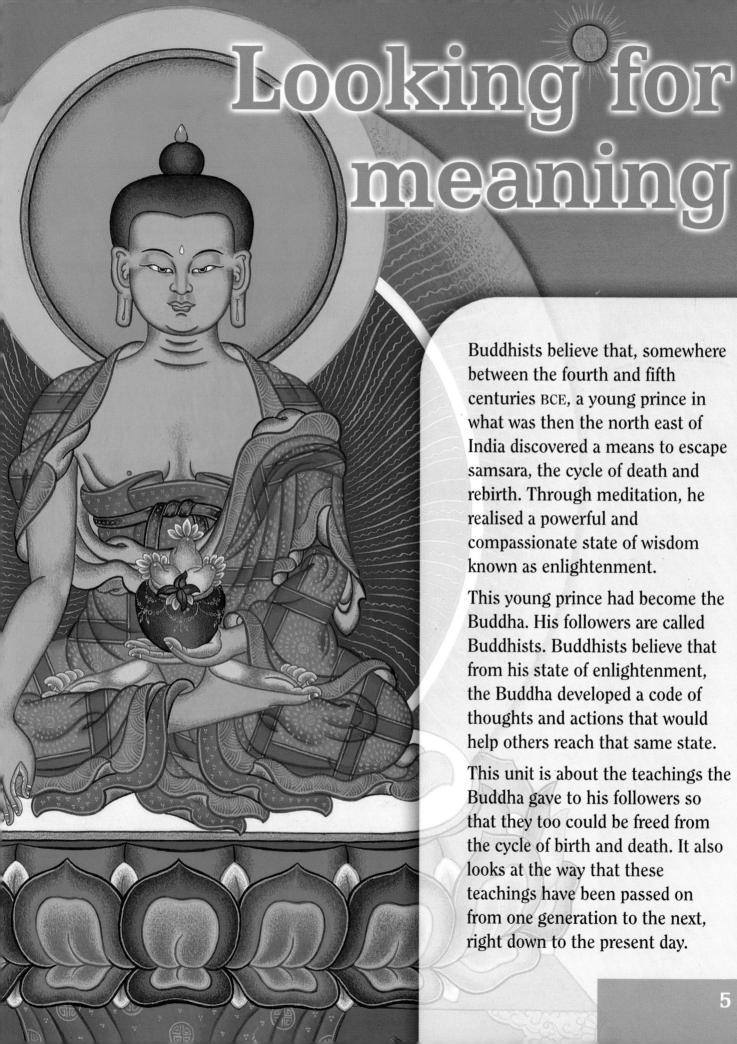

Looking for meaning

Buddhists believe that, somewhere between the fourth and fifth centuries BCE, a young prince in what was then the north east of India discovered a means to escape samsara, the cycle of death and rebirth. Through meditation, he realised a powerful and compassionate state of wisdom known as enlightenment.

This young prince had become the Buddha. His followers are called Buddhists. Buddhists believe that from his state of enlightenment, the Buddha developed a code of thoughts and actions that would help others reach that same state.

This unit is about the teachings the Buddha gave to his followers so that they too could be freed from the cycle of birth and death. It also looks at the way that these teachings have been passed on from one generation to the next, right down to the present day.

The Four Noble Truths

Two and a half thousand years ago in north east India, a young prince called Siddhartha Gotama was suddenly struck by how much suffering there was in the world. He grew up surrounded by only pleasure with a life of luxury of which even the richest person in the world today might be jealous. One day, Siddhartha decided to see what lay beyond the palace walls, walls he had not gone beyond for all of his childhood and youth.

Four sights Siddhartha saw outside shocked him so deeply that they changed the course of his life. These were:

- an old man, bent double with age
- a sick man, riddled with disease
- a dead body
- a holy man.

Siddhartha was horrified. He suddenly realised the awful fact that we all grow old, get sick, and then die. Only the thought of the holy man gave him any shred of comfort. Siddhartha became obsessed with the question of how to make his life meaningful. In the end, he decided to leave his family and all his riches and to devote himself to finding out the answer to why we suffer.

A The four sights.

Having spent years searching for the answer, Siddhartha finally decided he would sit down under a tree and not get up again until he had found the answer. Terrifying demons and temptresses tried to stop him from reaching his goal but Siddhartha remained undistracted until, finally, he achieved a state completely beyond suffering. Buddhists call his experience an 'awakening' or '**enlightenment**'. Siddhartha Gotama came to be called the **Buddha**, which means 'the awakened one'.

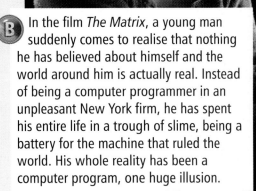

1 People in the West often have privileged lives. We don't see much death or many of the upsetting things about old age – it's usually hidden away from us. Write a modern-day version of Siddhartha's story set in this country, or design the storyboard for a short film of the story. Who's son might Siddhartha be? What sights might he see?

The Buddha's awakening

The Buddha had his awakening when he had realised four important things. He called these things the **Four Noble Truths**.

1 All beings suffer.
2 Suffering has a cause and that cause is '**craving**'.
3 It is possible to escape suffering.
4 There is a path to freedom from suffering.

What is real?

The path to the end of suffering explains that nothing is real and that the self that does the craving in Noble Truth 2 is nothing more than an idea.

Try thinking this through: everything is constantly moving and changing. By the time you finish reading this sentence, nothing in the universe will be exactly the same as it was when you started. Nothing is fixed – not even you. Your cells die and are replaced. Your thoughts flit from one thing to another, and you change your views over time. Think back to yourself two years ago. Are you truly the same person? Nothing is permanent, nothing is real. So the Buddha came to an amazing conclusion: there are no real, permanent objects and there is no real, permanent 'self'. There is no 'me'.

B In the film *The Matrix*, a young man suddenly comes to realise that nothing he has believed about himself and the world around him is actually real. Instead of being a computer programmer in an unpleasant New York firm, he has spent his entire life in a trough of slime, being a battery for the machine that ruled the world. His whole reality has been a computer program, one huge illusion.

The Buddha said people suffered because they didn't see things as they really were. Buddhists call this **ignorance**. It doesn't mean being stupid: it's just not knowing the truth about things. What the Buddha saw all around him were people desperately looking for ways to make themselves happy. People fought for wealth and power, worked all hours to buy nice things for themselves – but none of it brought lasting happiness. They were trying to grab hold of something they could cling to for support in an ever-changing universe. The Buddha, on the other hand, realised that true happiness came from letting everything go.

2 a What do you think the Buddha's friends might have said to him when he told them nothing was real? What might his argument have been in reply?

b Is there anything that's guaranteed to make people happy in life? Who is the happiest person you know? Describe what you think makes them happy.

Being the best you can be!

objective

to get to grips with the concepts of **rebirth** and samsara, to understand what different Buddhists believe about our human potential, to understand key human qualities of love and compassion

glossary

Arhat
Compassion
Dharma
Love
Mahayana
Rebirth
Samsara
Theravada

A Who said, 'It's a dog's life'?

Being a human is a pretty big deal. Scientists tell us that our planet has never seen anything like us before. No other animal can think, plan, reason and adapt like we can. We are not all-powerful, we are not perfect. But we are on a different level to all other life on earth.

Buddhists believe that when we die, we are reborn. This could be as an animal, or a human, or some other life-form. Buddhists call this process of being reborn again and again **samsara**. Samsara means 'to cycle' or 'go round'.

Buddhists see human birth as being very special. The Buddha showed that all life is suffering – no matter where you get reborn, you find suffering. Humans, though, have a great opportunity. If they follow the path the Buddha discovered, they can escape the cycle of birth and death altogether.

The Buddha said:

> *Rare is birth as a human being. Hard is the life of mortals. Hard it is to obtain the chance to listen to the Dharma. Rare is the appearance of the Buddhas.*

Activity

1 Most people joke that they'd like to come back as a cat because their cats seem to have such nice lives. What would a pet cat's life really be like? Would it be better or worse than a human's? Make a list of things that would be better and things that would be worse. Which side won for you?

One big family

Although humans have special opportunities, the Buddha taught that all beings are part of one big family. Every living thing has been reborn countless times, so any living thing you meet has been a relative or friend of yours in a previous life.

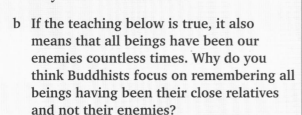

2 a Describe how you feel when you meet someone new for the first time. What things would make you like the person? What would switch you off them? Then describe how a Buddhist might feel when they meet someone new.

b If the teaching below is true, it also means that all beings have been our enemies countless times. Why do you think Buddhists focus on remembering all beings having been their close relatives and not their enemies?

The Buddha said:

One cannot count the number of times one being has been our mother.

Love and compassion

Because of the Buddha's teaching, Buddhists do not divide the world into 'us' and 'them'. Buddhists wish for everyone to be happy. A Buddhist prayer asks that 'May everyone be happy'. This wish is what Buddhists call **love**.

For Buddhists, happiness is being free from suffering. So Buddhists also try to have **compassion** for all living beings. This means they wish that they could also be free of suffering.

Two Buddhist traditions

There are two main types of Buddhism: the **Mahayana** tradition and the **Theravada** tradition. Around 80 per cent of the world's Buddhists are Mahayanists and 20 per cent are Theravadins. These two groups of Buddhists have lots in common, but there are also some differences. For example:

- In both traditions, Buddhists believe that being reborn again and again is suffering. Theravadins believe that each individual must try to escape from samsara for themselves. So Theravada Buddhists try to bring their own suffering to an end. Someone who does this is called an **arhat** or 'noble one'.
- Mahayana Buddhists try to become Buddhas themselves. Just as the Buddha found the end to suffering but stayed on earth to help others, these Buddhists aim to be just like him, returning to the world again and again to help free others from suffering.

3 a For a couple of minutes, close your eyes and think 'May everyone be happy'. Start with friends and family, then strangers, then even people you don't like that much. Write down how it felt. Describe what was difficult about it.

b List the things that you think make humans special. What things would a Buddhist list?

c Both Theravada and Mahayana Buddhists follow the Buddha's example. How would you explain the difference between them?

Going for refuge

objective

to look at the Three Jewels of Refuge and consider the ways Buddhists try to escape suffering

glossary

Refuge
Sangha
Three Jewels of
    Refuge

A The woman in this picture is a refugee. She has escaped from a country torn apart by war and suffering. The picture shows her being welcomed to safety by a friend in this country.

The Buddha taught that all beings experience suffering. For Buddhists, the first step to escaping from this suffering is to 'go for **refuge**'. A refuge is a place of safety. When people escape from suffering in their own country to live in a safer place, we call them refugees.

B

1 a The three people in **B** are all looking to escape from their suffering. Describe what is happening in each cartoon, and where these people might go to for help.

  b Could this help solve their problems permanently or only for a while?

Buddhists have three places they can go to for help. These are called the **Three Jewels of Refuge**.

The first jewel: the Buddha

The first refuge is the Buddha. The Buddha showed people the way out of suffering. The first line of the refuge prayer is: 'I go for refuge to the Buddha.' This is like asking the Buddha to act as a guide, to guide the person out of suffering.

The second jewel: the dharma

Even though Buddhists believe the Buddha has the power to guide them, they also believe that they cannot just rely on him to do all the work for them. After all, if you want to escape from danger, you need to follow your guide's instructions! The Buddha's instructions on how to escape suffering are called the dharma. Dharma is an Indian word that means 'truth'.

Just as the Buddha is thought of like a guide, his teachings are like a map that shows the path out of suffering. When Buddhists say 'I go for refuge to the dharma', they are saying they have complete faith in the power of the Buddha's teaching to lead them out of suffering.

The third jewel: the sangha

The **sangha** is the Buddhist community. It includes both those Buddhists who have understood the deeper meanings of the Buddha's teachings and, more generally, all those who follow the Buddha's teachings. They are like a Buddhist's companions on the path away from suffering.

For Buddhists, saying 'I go for refuge to the sangha' means that they are going to spend their time with people who follow the Buddha's teaching because they want to think and be like them.

2 Does who you are with influence how you behave?

a On paper or in your folder, write *two* descriptions of the boy in **C** to go in *two* empty speech bubbles: one from his gran and one from the policewoman.

b Which description do you think the boy would say was most like the real him? Why does who you are with influence how you are?

c Why might Buddhists want to go for refuge to the sangha when they already have the Buddha and his teachings to help them?

3 Why do you think Buddhists call the three refuges 'jewels'?

Life after death (after life, after death, after life...)

objective

to think through what the Buddha said happens when you die, to understand what science says about energy and to explore the Buddhist concept of karma

glossary

Karma

Buddhists believe that at death the mind leaves the body and then, depending on the belief in a 'self' and how it has behaved in the past, rebirth happens.

Activity

1 What do you think happens when you die? Which *one* of the four views in **A** is most like yours?

A

My nan died five years ago, but I still feel she is with me sometimes. I believe your spirit lives on after death.

What happens when you die?

I believe life is the same as all energy: it never ends, it just passes from one living thing to another.

I know that there is a heaven. I know God through my prayers. I hope I will go to heaven when I die.

There is no life but this one. When you die, that's it. What's important is making the most of your life now.

Many people might think that the idea of rebirth is about as far from modern-day science as you can get, but Buddhists would disagree. A fundamental law of science is:

> Energy cannot be created or destroyed; it can only be transformed.
>
> Sir Issac Newton

This means that the amount of energy in the universe is always the same. All that happens is that this energy is changed from one form to another. For example, when you eat something, what you eat becomes part of you and the calories it contains fuel your body. You are changing one form of energy (e.g. a chocolate bar) into another (e.g. a crazy dance move). Can you say, then, that anything ever really dies, if it actually just goes on to be something else?

Karma

Just as Buddhists believe in rebirth, they also believe that all actions have results. Good acts bring good results and bad acts bring bad results. Buddhists use a word, **karma**, to describe this. Karma means action. Karma is like another scientific concept, called 'cause and effect'. This means one thing makes something else happen.

For Buddhists, karma is built up over lifetimes. Your actions in this life influence what your next life will be like. However, you also have karma built up from lots of previous lifetimes so you might be starting this life with a lot of baggage to deal with, or you might be very well set up by previous lifetimes filled with good karma.

The Buddha said:

> What we are today comes from our thoughts of yesterday, and our present thoughts build our life of tomorrow.

B

Activity

2 a Study picture **B**. Imagine that this is all the same water, in these three different forms. How might a Buddhist use these three images to explain samsara?

  b Buddhists believe the mind leaves the body at death and because of karma and the belief in a 'self' rebirth happens. What does 'mind' mean for you? Could it be the same as energy – something that can be transformed into something else?

Activity

3 a Write, draw or act out a story in which someone's actions cause a bad result and a good result.

  b Does it matter if you do something bad but no one ever finds out? How would a Buddhist answer this question?

  c What actions would make you proud of the way you have lived your life? Draw up a list of things you would like to do for other people. Build in the Buddhist ideas of love and compassion as you do this.

The Buddhist wheel of life

objective

to recognise some of the important symbols drawn in the Buddhist wheel of life

glossary

Nirvana
Realm
Visual aid

Picture **A** is of the Buddhist wheel of life. At 2,300 years old, the wheel of life is one of the world's oldest **visual aids**.

The three poisons

At the very centre of the wheel are three animals: a pig; a snake; and a pigeon. These animals are symbols of three ways of thinking.

The pig is a symbol for ignorance or 'not knowing'. The Buddha taught that ignorance is not knowing that nothing stays the same, nothing is real, there is no permanent 'self' – no real 'me'.

Out of the pig's mouth come a pigeon and a snake. The pigeon is a symbol of desire (wanting things). The snake is a symbol of hate. They come out of the pig's mouth to show that desire for things and hatred of things both come out of ignorance.
Buddhists believe there are actually no real 'things' to desire or hate.

> 2 a What animals (or other symbols) might you use instead of the three shown in picture **A**? Why?
>
>   b Sometimes Buddhists call ignorance, desire and hatred the 'three poisons'. Why do you think they call them poisons?

> 1 Symbols are shortcuts to understanding bigger concepts. They are a quick way to get your meaning across. The symbol for Buddhism is the wheel. From what you already know about Buddhism, can you explain what this symbol stands for?

The two paths

Outside the central circle of the Buddhist wheel are two semi-circles – one white, one black. These are called:
- the white path of good karma
- the black path of bad karma.

Buddhists believe that good acts bring good results and bad acts bring bad results, and that this karma affects what happens in later rebirths. In picture A, there are three beings moving up on the white side:
- a human
- a demi-god (more than a human but less than a god)
- a god.

These show how good actions cause rebirth in the human **realm** of rebirth (good), the demi-god realm (better) or the god realm (better still).

The three beings moving down the black side are:
- an animal
- a ghost
- a hell being.

These symbolise how bad actions cause rebirth in the animal realm (not good), ghost realm (bad) or hell realm (even worse).

The six realms

Outside these semi-circles are six sections like cake slices. These are pictures of the six realms of rebirth (**B**):

The god realm: here, beings experience great pleasure but ultimately still experience the terrible suffering of losing all they have. This is the highest realm but it is not **nirvana**. People who lead a very good life but are rather proud of how good they are get reborn here.

The demi-god realm: these beings are constantly fighting and losing against the gods. This realm is the result of living a very good life but being jealous of others.

The human realm: People who lead a very good life but believe there is a permanent self are reborn here, and so experience all the sufferings of birth, old age, sickness and death.

The animal realm: if someone behaves stupidly, not thinking about the results of their actions, they are born as animals with the sufferings of being killed and eaten, or made into slaves.

The hungry ghost realm: if someone constantly wants things and is never satisfied, there is rebirth as a hungry ghost, living in deserts where there is no food or water for 15,000 years.

Hell realm: the cause of rebirth in hell is getting angry all the time. Here, beings suffer intense heat or cold for billions of years.

Each of the circles in the wheel of life is the cause of the next one. Because of the three poisons, beings create karma, which causes rebirth in one of the six realms of samsara.

The 12 links and the Lord of Death

The outer circle has 12 pictures that show how all the different sufferings in life happen because of ignorance.

The whole of the wheel is in the grip of Yama, the Lord of Death. This reminds Buddhists that death is a certainty in the cycle of samsara.

3 a Do you think the wheel of life helps you to understand Buddhism, or does it make it more complicated? State which aspects it helps explain, and which aspects are not clear.

b If you have a list of unanswered questions, try and find out the answers. You can send an e-mail to buddhism@nelsonthornes.com to ask a Buddhist for more information.

Buddhist scriptures

Religious people turn to **scriptures** – religious writings – to help them make important decisions in life. Scriptures are a **source of authority**: something you turn to when you need information you believe you can trust absolutely.

A Many people turn to the Internet as a source of authority.

Buddhism has many such writings, many of them based on the Buddha's own teachings. By the time these writings were written down, Buddhism had spread far and wide. Different ways of thinking about the Buddha and his teachings had developed. A split occurred and Buddhists today are either in the Theravada tradition or in the Mahayana tradition. Theravada and Mahayana Buddhists have different scriptures. They also share some scriptures, but sometimes draw different meanings from them.

The Theravada scriptures: The Tipitaka

Tipitaka means 'The Three Baskets'. These three sets of scriptures are believed by Theravadins to be genuine Buddhist teachings. They were first written on palm leaves which were kept in baskets.

Activity

1 a Not everything on the Internet can be trusted. Where would you look on the Internet for information you could trust?

b What makes the source trustworthy? List *five* reasons to trust a site and *five* reasons to be wary.

B

The **Vinaya** or 'discipline' basket
Sets of rules for different types of Buddhist. These include the rules for Buddhist monks to follow.

The **Sutta** or 'teachings' basket
Mainly the actual teachings of the Buddha; his words. Includes the Four Noble Truths and the **Noble Eightfold Path**.

The **Abhidhamma** or 'higher teachings' basket
Contains deeper teachings that explain what the universe and the person actually are by breaking them down into parts.

objective

to be introduced to the key scriptures in Buddhism, to understand how different traditions use different scriptures, and to consider why scriptures would be important for Buddhists

glossary

Abhidhamma
Meditation
Noble Eightfold
   Path
Scriptures
Source of authority
Sutra
Sutta
Tipitaka
Vinaya

2 Read diagram **B**.

  a What 'writings' would go into the discipline basket?

  b What 'writings' would go into the teachings basket? Would worksheets count? What else?

  c What would you classify as 'higher teachings'? These would be things that really made you understand what school was all about.

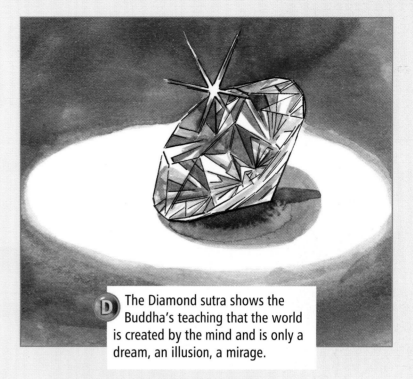

D The Diamond sutra shows the Buddha's teaching that the world is created by the mind and is only a dream, an illusion, a mirage.

The Mahayana scriptures

Mahayana Buddhists also have the Three Baskets. However, they have more **sutras** (the Mahayana word for sutta) which explain the path to the end of suffering and to enlightenment. Two important Mahayana scriptures are shown in diagrams **C** and **D**.

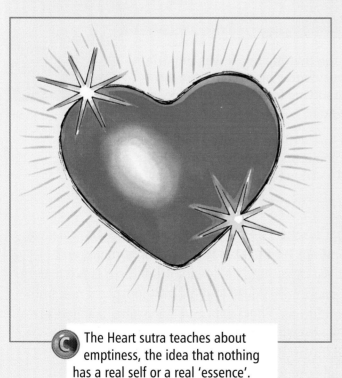

C The Heart sutra teaches about emptiness, the idea that nothing has a real self or a real 'essence'.

The importance of scripture

Buddhists believe their scriptures contain all the advice and instructions necessary to manage every aspect of their lives, both in formal religious circumstances and in everyday situations. The Vinaya acts as a map showing how to live and behave. Scripture is used in ritual, for prayer, as a **meditation** manual and a guide on what to think; it can be read to bring benefit to present and future lives. Buddhists keep their scriptures in a place of honour, often above a shrine containing an image of the Buddha.

3 a Heart and diamond: what do these words make you feel? Why do you think the sutras are called these things?

  b Zen Buddhism, in the Mahayana tradition, places more importance on each person's own experience rather than written scriptures. What do you think? Can a book teach you as much as life? Do you prefer detailed instructions or general suggestions?

17

Teachers are important!

objective

to understand why teachers are an important source of authority in Buddhism and to think through the concept of lineage in Mahayana Buddhism

glossary

Lama
Lineage

After the Buddha reached enlightenment, he began to help others. For 40 years he travelled far and wide, teaching people about the way to escape suffering. He said that he taught about just one thing: suffering and the end of suffering.

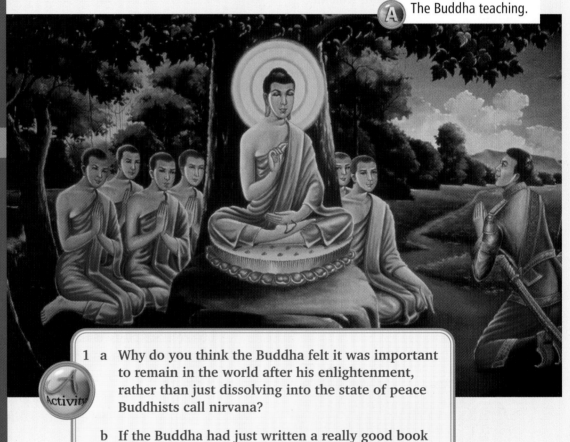

A The Buddha teaching.

1 a Why do you think the Buddha felt it was important to remain in the world after his enlightenment, rather than just dissolving into the state of peace Buddhists call nirvana?

b If the Buddha had just written a really good book for others to read about his discovery, would that have been as good as travelling around teaching?

Buddhists believe that teachers are very important. Teachers will clear up any misunderstandings or mistakes learners might make, and explain things that need explaining. Following Buddhism is not like swotting to pass an exam. It is a deep and difficult journey. So in both the main Buddhist traditions, Theravada and Mahayana, teachers are important sources of authority.

- In Theravada Buddhism, the word for teacher means 'elder'.
- In Mahayana Buddhism, the word means 'spiritual friend'.
- In a Tibetan type of Mahayana Buddhism, teachers are called **lama** (like the Dalai Lama). Students try to think of their lama as an actual Buddha and pray to him or her for blessings.

2 a Do you think it's best to see your teacher as a friend or an elder? List the advantages and disadvantages of each.

b What would a perfect teacher be like for you? Draw a picture of what they would look like and label all their excellent features, or write 'a perfect teacher' in the middle of a page and create a spider diagram listing their qualities around the outside.

c Now describe what a perfect teacher might be like for a Buddhist. Use the same method to present your answer.

What makes a good teacher?

Scriptures in each tradition have long, complicated lists of the qualifications of a proper teacher. In brief, the person should keep the vows of his or her tradition properly, and have real experience of the meaning of the teaching. A Buddhist might say that if you are going to climb a dangerous mountain, it's good to have a guide who has climbed it already.

In the Tibetan Buddhist tradition, there is something else that gives the teacher authority: the 'blessing of the **lineage**'. A lineage is like an unbroken chain running back through history. Each link in the chain is a teacher. Each teacher taught the next teacher in the chain. Each, in turn, received a teaching from their master, learned to understand it, then passed it on to their student for him or her to do the same. Tibetan Buddhists believe that the lineage of a teacher is very important. Teachings without a lineage would be thought of as having lost their power.

This kind of tradition in teaching has been very important as Buddhism has come to new cultures. In Western countries, for example, the culture is very different from traditional Buddhist lands. The lineage of teachers helps keep the core of Buddhism intact. It also helps students know where a teacher is coming from.

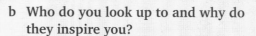
This is Milarepa, a Tibetan saint, who lived 1040–1123 CE. Milarepa actually killed people in his youth, but his teacher's lineage was so strong that he overcame such terrible actions to reach enlightenment. Milarepa's life story has inspired many generations of Tibetans. Why do you think this is?

3 a Successful sports stars often go into teaching as they get older. Give *three* or more reasons why young hopefuls might want to be coached by them.

b Who do you look up to and why do they inspire you?

c Tibetan Buddhists coming to the West for the first time would experience a very different culture. Write a postcard from a young Tibetan student back to their lama in Asia, describing their visit to your school. How would they describe the teachers and students here?

Buddhism and science

In the West, we usually see religion and science in conflict: most of us think science is about facts you can prove, and religions are about beliefs that you can't.

For many centuries, for example, Christian leaders taught that the world had been created by God in seven days. One bishop even used information in the Bible to date creation to 4,004 years before the birth of Christ, on the 26 October, at 9 o'clock in the morning.

As scientific understanding developed, scientists started to challenge this view.

- Geologists proved that the earth was millions of years old, not thousands.
- Biologists developed the theory of **evolution**, proving that life on earth had not all been created in one go, and that humans only evolved very recently.
- Cosmologists, studying the history of the universe, discovered that everything is rushing at tremendous speed away from one central point.

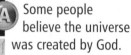

A Some people believe the universe was created by God.

The Big Bang

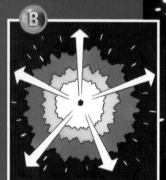

In 1948, a scientist called George Gamow put forward an explanation for how the universe was created: the theory of the '**Big Bang**'. In the beginning there was nothing but a tiny point of matter, incredibly dense and hot. This exploded outwards, creating the universe as it did so. It is still expanding now.

The Big Bang, Big Crunch, Big Bang

Other scientists questioned this theory – where did the original tiny point of matter come from? Maybe, they thought, at some point an expanding universe runs out of 'push'. Just like a ball thrown up in the air, there's a point where gravity starts to pull it back down again. From that point on, the universe rushes in on itself, until, finally, it all crunches back together again into a tiny point of matter. Then, who knows? Maybe the whole process starts again with another Big Bang, so the whole universe is created and destroyed, created and destroyed in an endless cycle.

objective

to evaluate the connections between modern scientific viewpoints and Buddhist viewpoints about the universe

glossary

Big Bang
Evolution
Multiverse

Universe or multiverse

If this wasn't enough to deal with, a scientist called M J Murcott asked an interesting question: 'Is there just one universe?' Maybe, instead of one universe, endlessly being created and destroyed, there are an infinite number of them, each at different stages in the Big Bang/Big Crunch process. He called this limitless collection of universes the **multiverse**.

Buddhism also teaches that there are many realms and dimensions (see pages 14–15), which would fit with scientific theories about multiverses. According to Buddhist theory, rebirth after death can happen in one of lots of different realms, depending on the balance of good or bad karma. Although humans cannot see the hell realm or god realm, for example, they could easily be in other dimensions.

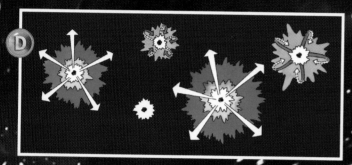

D

The Buddhist theory of universal creation

Nearly 3,000 years ago, Buddhist beliefs about an infinite number of universes were first written down. Buddhism teaches that each universe has four ages:

1 Creation.
2 Existence.
3 Destruction.
4 Emptiness.

At the end of the age of existence, the universe begins to dissolve into the age of destruction. When that comes to an end, the only physical thing that remains is the place where the Buddha achieved enlightenment. This place is sometimes called the 'Indestructible Seat'. This is the beginning of the age of emptiness. When that comes to an end, a new age of creation begins. The process is said to have no beginning or end.

E Buddhist monks at Bodhgaya – the 'Indestructible Seat'.

Activity

1 Buddhist understanding of the universe shows some similarities with scientific ideas. List *three* connections between them.

2 Design a poster to show the *four* ages of Buddhist creation.

3 A video game company is interested in a new role-play game set in a Buddhist multiverse. The designer needs a brief for four dimensions: these will be the four levels of the game.

   a Write a description for *four* realms of rebirth: landscape and inhabitants required.

   b Explain how karma points are earned in the game. There should be both good and bad karma points.

   c Work out how the main character's karma points determine which realm their life-force is reborn into.

The religion of the future will be a cosmic religion. It should transcend a personal god and avoid dogmas and theology. Covering both the natural and the spiritual, it should be based on a religious sense arising from the experience of all things, natural and spiritual as a meaningful unity. If there is any religion that would cope with modern scientific needs, it would be Buddhism.

Albert Einstein

Search for truth

Meditation and the search for truth

The Buddha taught that enlightenment came from within a person, not from blindly following someone else's rules or from believing in a god. Buddhists believe we have all the answers to life's big questions within us.

When the Buddha started on his search for the truth, he used meditation to help him – a set of techniques for concentrating and focusing the mind. His teachers were amazed at how quickly he progressed through more and more difficult stages. Through meditation, the Buddha eventually reached enlightenment. Buddhists since have followed his approach.

Most non-Buddhists think of meditation as a way of relaxing and de-stressing. Buddhists describe the human mind as being like a monkey swinging through the trees, grabbing at one branch after another.

Calming meditation

Buddhists use meditation techniques to produce a feeling of calm and stillness. This is done by focusing on something – like your breathing, just concentrating on the feeling of breathing in and out or counting your breaths. It takes a while to learn but, eventually, people can learn not to be distracted by the 'mind chatter' going on in their heads. This feels very peaceful and tranquil.

Insight meditation

Calming meditation is very important in Buddhism, but only as a first step. Once Buddhists have mastered it, they go on to practice another exercise called **insight meditation**. Once you have calmed your mind, you can really start to concentrate and find things out about yourself. The Buddha discovered **Three Universal Truths** through insight meditation called **anicca**, **anatta** and **dukkha**.

objective

to understand how Buddhists search for truth through meditation. To consider the Buddhist concepts of anicca, dukkha and anatta. To understand some differences in the way Buddhists turn to the Buddha for help.

glossary

Anatta
Anicca
Bodhisattva
Dukkha
Insight meditation
Three Universal
    Truths

1 a Close your eyes and try not to follow your thoughts about anything for one minute.

b Describe what happened and what you think Buddhists mean about the monkeys!

Anicca, anatta, and dukkha – impermanence, no-self and suffering

Anicca is about everything changing. Looking at his mind, the Buddha saw how thoughts and feelings flitted across it like constantly changing clouds passing through a clear blue sky.

Anatta means 'no-self'. Deep in meditation, the Buddha found a place underneath his thoughts where all personal issues and needs fell away. He realised that there was no real 'me' and/or 'mine', that these were all just thoughts projected on to an ever-changing universe.

Dukkha means suffering or dissatisfaction. Concentrating deeply, the Buddha had the insight that suffering is everywhere because we take everything as being 'real', and that we take everything as real because we don't recognise how things change all the time.

Many Theravadin Buddhists use insight meditation on anicca, anatta and dukkha to try and experience these three realisations for themselves and escape suffering.

2 a Some religions say followers should have faith that what they teach is the truth. How would you say Buddhism is different?

b Do you believe that Everest is the tallest mountain in the world? If so, have you measured it yourself? Why might some religious believers use this example to explain faith? What might the Buddha reply to this argument?

Communicating with the Buddha

Buddhists turn to the Buddha for help in their search for truth. They do this in different ways. They meditate in front of a picture or statue of a Buddha and place offerings in front of it.

These actions have different meanings in the different types of Buddhism. The main difference is that in Mahayana Buddhism people pray to the Buddha and Buddhist 'saints', called **bodhisattvas**, to help them become enlightened. Theravada Buddhists, though, do not pray in this way. They make offerings in front of images of the historical Buddha, Siddhartha Gotama, to help focus their minds on what he achieved. They also make offerings because giving is good karma.

3 a When people leave flowers to remember a dead person, it is to honour and remember that person. It is not because they think the dead person will like them. How could you use this statement to explain how some Buddhists make offerings on shrines to the Buddha?

b Pictures can be very powerful and inspirational. Design a poster featuring something or someone you find inspirational. You might wish to add some words.

Many people in this country turn to meditation to help them deal with stressful situations. This Theravada monastery in Hertfordshire runs weekend courses in meditation for anyone to attend.

Assessment for Unit 1

Life after death, sources of authority

After six years of studying and meditating, Siddhartha Gotama decided to sit down under a tree and not move until he reached his goal of perfection. 'Even if my body dries up and my skin, flesh and bones fall away, I will not move until I have reached enlightenment.' Terrified that he might achieve it, the Buddhist equivalent of the devil, Mara, sent different disturbing visions to distract Siddhartha Gotama from his goal. However, even though thunder roared and the earth shook, Siddhartha Gotama could not be distracted and remained focused and purposeful. Eventually, with Mara subdued, Siddhartha Gotama overcame the last traces of ignorance and achieved the state of perfect enlightenment.

These questions test different sets of skills in RE. Which skills do you need to work on? Choose the level you need and work through the tasks set.

Level 3

- Look at the picture of the Buddha. Describe the different ways you can see in which Mara tried to prevent him from becoming enlightened and the different ways in which the Buddha overcame the problems.
- Buddhists say the best 'weapon' for defeating enemies is patience. What do you think they mean by this? Say why you agree or disagree with them.
- Buddhists rely on the Buddha's teachings to help guide them through life. Who or what do you rely on to guide you?

Level 4

- Describe *three* sources of authority a Buddhist could turn to if they wanted to know what was right or wrong.
- Choose another religion and try to think of *three* sources of authority a follower of that faith could turn to.
- What *three* sources of authority would you turn to if you wanted to know something? Explain which you value most and why.

Level 5

- Describe what Buddhists think about what happens after death.
- How do Buddhist ideas about life after death differ from Christian ones? Are there any similarities?
- Make up a question you could ask a Buddhist about life after death. Now say how you think he or she might answer it.

Level 6

- Give a detailed explanation of the Four Noble Truths.
- Explain some of the similarities and differences between the Theravada and Mahayana Buddhist traditions.
- List some ways that beliefs in rebirth and karma might affect a Buddhist living in today's world.

Who is responsible?

CHANEL

Der Krämer.

People often think of religion as being something very private, a purely personal thing. Prayer and meditation are seen as solitary activities in an inner world that people on the 'outside' can't see.

But religion doesn't just affect people's 'inner worlds'. As well as influencing how they think, a person's beliefs often affect the way they speak to others and the way they interact with other people. This happens at a global scale too: just try listening to the news for half an hour without religion getting a mention!

In this unit we will start to look at the social side of Buddhism: its teachings on how people should relate to others. Instead of grasping at selfish things, Buddhists try to focus on achieving real happiness that lasts. Like the painter of this skeleton picture, Buddhists try to remember that thinking about others makes a meaningful life, while thinking about yourself just leads to wasting it!

The Noble Eightfold Path

objective

to think through the Buddha's teachings on making the right choices in life

glossary

Buddha
Four Noble Truths
Karma
Meditation
Nirvana
Noble Eightfold
    Path
Rebirth
Three Universal
    Truths

The **Buddha's** message was straightforward: there is suffering and there is an end to suffering. What was not so simple was how to follow his path and escape from suffering.

The **Noble Eightfold Path** consists of eight ways of thinking, speaking and behaving that the Buddha said people should follow if they want to reach the end of suffering, **nirvana**.

A Noble Eightfold Path.

Right understanding

This means understanding the Buddha's teachings on **karma** and **rebirth**, the **Three Universal Truths** and the **Four Noble Truths**. However, this is not just understanding what they mean; rather, it is where you actually feel those things to be true in your heart and how they influence the way you see and do things every day.

Right intention

Right intention means doing things for the right reasons – the right intentions. Instead of thinking about doing things for oneself, a Buddhist thinks about doing things for others. Instead of thinking about how they can harm others, Buddhists think about how they can help others. Basically, right intention is developing the wish to stop doing things for bad reasons and, instead, do them for good reasons.

Right speech

Right speech means: (1) not lying; (2) not swearing; (3) not gossiping; and (4) not saying things that cause other people to fall out. A Buddhist always tries to tell the truth, to speak pleasantly and about meaningful subjects. Finally, he or she tries to speak in ways that cause harmony between people.

Right action

Right action means: (1) not killing or injuring any living being; (2) not stealing; and (3) not committing sexual misconduct (this means not having sex with someone else's partner).

Right livelihood

A Buddhist must never make their living in a way that is harmful to others. This means that he or she can never work selling: (1) weapons; (2) meat; (3) slaves; (4) harmful drugs; or (5) poisons. A Buddhist could be a chemist because the drugs he/she sold would not harm people. They could not own a pub though!

Right effort

Right effort means making an effort to abandon negative ways of thinking such as proud, angry, or jealous thoughts and, instead, making an effort to develop positive ways of thinking such as humble, generous or compassionate thoughts.

Right mindfulness

To be mindful of something means to remember it. We all have mindfulness but it is usually mindfulness of something meaningless like the pop song we can't stop singing or the girl or boy we can't stop thinking about. Buddhists learn to be mindful of a calm and peaceful state of mind so that when something that causes a strong sense of 'self' suddenly appears to the mind, be it a thought, a feeling, a sensation, or an object, they remember or are 'mindful' of that calm and peaceful state of mind.

Right concentration

Right concentration is the ability to keep the mind totally concentrated on a calm, peaceful state without becoming distracted. It is very similar to right mindfulness, indeed the two work together very closely. While right concentration remains focused on the calm and peaceful state, right mindfulness notices when the mind starts to get distracted and pulls it back to the object of concentration.

By keeping the mind concentrated through right concentration, and using right mindfulness to stop being distracted, a Buddhist gradually dissolves their mind into deeper and deeper states of **meditation** until eventually they reach nirvana. Here, because they have gone beyond the sense of 'self', they achieve the end to suffering.

1 Do you think it would be easy to follow the Noble Eightfold Path? Which part of the Path would be most difficult and why?

Sometimes it is said that while the first three Noble Truths are Buddhist philosophy, the fourth Noble Truth makes Buddhism a religion. This is because, while the first three Noble Truths talk about how things are, the fourth Noble Truth, the Path, actually tells you how to be.

2 Design a snakes and ladder game to help explain the ideas of the Noble Eightfold Path to young Buddhists. The last square should be nirvana. Use real-life situations that young children will be familiar with to help them get to grips with things.

You should have ladders for doing the right thing, for example:

- other children were calling someone nasty names but you wouldn't join in

- your meditation class went really well: your teacher is pleased with how well you concentrated.

You should have snakes for bad actions, for example:

- you have forgotten the Four Noble Truths: go back five squares

- you squash a fly on purpose.

The ten negative actions

objective

to understand how
the ten negative
actions show
Buddhists how to
behave in order to
reduce their
suffering

glossary

Ignorance
Realm
Scriptures
Ten negative
   actions

The Noble Eightfold Path and Buddhist **scriptures** in general show Buddhists the things they should try to do to reduce suffering – and to escape suffering altogether. The Buddha also taught that there are **ten negative actions** that cause beings to suffer: Buddhists should try very hard not to do them.

The ten negative actions are made up of three that are done with the body, four that are done by speech and three that are done with the mind (see diagram **A**).

1 a Write down as many of your school rules as you can remember. How many of them tell you what to do, and how many tell you what not to do?

   b All religions have rules about what believers should and should not do. Do you think it is easier to follow rules that tell you what not to do, or rules that tell you what to aim for?

A

Body
Killing.
Stealing.
Sex with
someone else's
partner.

Speech
Lying.
Saying things that hurt people.
Saying things that cause
division between people.
Gossiping.

Mind
Harmful thoughts.
Wishing that something that belongs
to someone else belonged to you.
'Holding wrong views': not
believing in karma, the Buddhist
teachings, etc.

2 Write a rough script layout for a soap opera in which the three main characters commit as many of the ten negative actions as possible. Other scriptwriters will put in the dialogue: they just need a brief guide on the story line.

3 Which of the ten negative actions are caused by anger, which by desire, and which by ignorance? Some might be caused by more than one. Use a Venn diagram like the one shown in **B** to sort the ten negative actions into the three groups and show where there could be overlap.

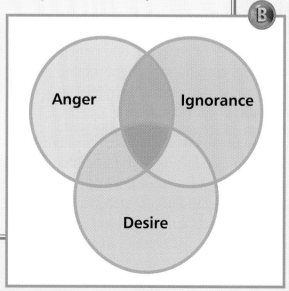

B

Anger   Ignorance

Desire

The results of negative actions

The centre of the Buddhist wheel of life.

Each negative action has four types of negative results. Some of these have quite complicated names!

① Rebirth into the three lower realms

Actions caused by anger lead to rebirth in hell, those caused by desire lead to rebirth as a ghost, and **ignorance** causes rebirth as an animal.

② The effect similar to the cause

Karma builds up over many lifetimes. A murderer will be reborn in the hell **realm**, but this time in hell doesn't last forever – millions of years, but not forever. Once the former murderer is reborn as a human again, this human life will only be a short one. The cause of negative karma was the murder, and the effect is that the murderer's next human life is cut short, just like the murdered person's was.

> **Activity**
>
> 4 Pick out *four* more negative actions and try to imagine what 'the effect similar to the cause' might be in each case.

③ The continued tendency

This means that if you have stolen in this life, you will have the habit of stealing in the next life. In other words, each time you do a negative action, it makes it that much easier to do it again.

> **Activity**
>
> 5 a Habits can be hard to break. What advice would you give someone who is trying to break a bad habit?
>
> b Some Buddhists would say that it is more important to stop doing things because of 'the continued tendency' rather than the risk of rebirth into one of the lower realms. Why might they think this?

④ The environmental effect

The environmental effect is about the conditions you live in. Killing, for example, is said to cause rebirth in a hostile place, such as a war zone, and stealing causes rebirth in a place where it is difficult to find the basic necessities of life.

> **Activity**
>
> 6 a Look at the two photos shown in **D**. How would a Buddhist explain that these two children were born into such different worlds?
>
> b How would the Buddhist explanation change how you felt about children living in war zones or famine areas?

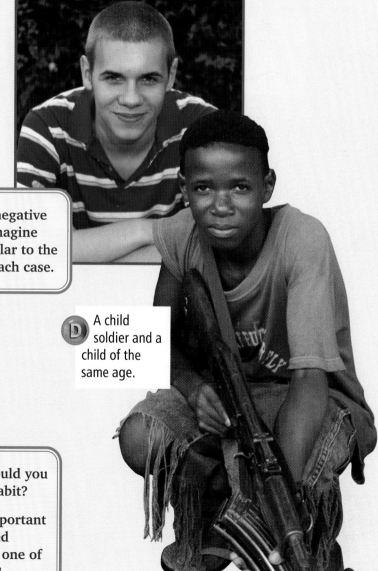

D A child soldier and a child of the same age.

Family life

objective

to understand what the Buddha taught families about how to live life

glossary

Desire
Love
Mahayana

Close your eyes for a moment and see what picture comes to mind when you think of the word 'Buddhism'.

 Which one of these people is a Buddhist? How can you tell?

Most people think Buddhism means a man in robes, sat under a tree, meditating. What most people probably wouldn't think of would be a couple with children, living an ordinary family life.

While most people seem to think of Buddhism as a religion of monks, the truth is that the Buddha gave many teachings during his life: some to fit the needs of monks and nuns; and others to fit the needs of those who choose to live an ordinary family lifestyle.

For example, the Buddha said:

> Supporting your parents,
> Caring for your wife and children,
> And having a peaceful occupation;
> This is the highest blessing.

1 Is family life a blessing? What do you think? With a partner, brainstorm the advantages and disadvantages of:

a living on your own

b family life.

Now say which *one* you would prefer and why.

For Buddhists, a relationship should have a foundation of love. But this is not the 'love' most people think of when the word is mentioned, where you can't stop thinking about how wonderful someone is and feel that you would be happy forever if you could be with them. Buddhists call that 'desire'. Buddhist love, on the other hand, is a strong feeling of wanting others to be happy, like the feeling a mother has for her child. So, while one kind of 'love' thinks about one's own happiness, Buddhist love thinks about the other person's happiness.

2 Explain the *two* kinds of love described above to a partner, especially the differences between them. Now write down what you said and share it with others.

The duties of a couple

The Buddha gave advice on how a husband and wife should treat each other.

> There are five ways in which a husband should care for his wife...:
> By respecting her, not criticising her, not being unfaithful to her,
> By giving her authority (in the home), by providing her with gifts.
> And, there are five ways in which a wife... should pay him back:
> By doing her duties well, by treating his family as her own,
> By not being unfaithful, by protecting the family's belongings,
> And by being skilful and hard working in all that she does.

3 a Some people might say that the Buddha's advice was a little old fashioned, while others might see no need to change it. If anything needs updating, what would you change and how would you change it?

   b Imagine you are a member of a committee set up to help strengthen family life in twenty-first century society. Your job is to produce a set of *10* rules for how a couple should treat one another.

The Mahayana Buddhist view – All one big family

In the **Mahayana** Buddhist tradition of Tibet, China and Japan the idea of seeing all beings as part of one huge family is really important. The third Dalai Lama said:

> There is no being we can say has not been our parent. In fact, each and every being has been our parent countless times.

In Mahayana Buddhism, people commit to becoming a Buddha so they can free all beings from suffering. Seeing all beings as having been close relatives is the first step for Mahayana Buddhists.

4 Think back to an argument you had recently with someone who isn't part of your family. Now imagine what effect it would have if you suddenly discovered that they were your long-lost brother or sister. How would your feelings change? Write a story to describe what would happen.

B Why isn't this the best way to solve a problem?

31

Buddhism blog: Yeshe Bahamon

Yeshe's Blog

Ⓐ This is me making offerings at our shrine at home.

About me

Name: Yeshe Bahamon

Age: 13 years old

Interests: PS2, gaming, running, skateboarding

Favourite music: Black Eyed Peas, Kanye West, Eminem

Favourite books: *The Magician*, *Lord of the Rings*, *Harry Potter*

Being a Buddhist

I pray and meditate every day and sometimes at weekends I go to the temple to pray with other people. Once a month we do group prayers to Padmasambhava or 'Guru Rinpoche'. I like this because we get lots of sweets and things. Two or three times a year the **lama** (a Tibetan word for a Buddhist teacher) gives teachings in Bristol or London so I go there with my mum and dad. Then, just after Christmas, he gives five days of teachings in Manchester on special Buddhist texts.

When I was a bit younger, I never used to go to these because I thought they were boring. Now that I'm older, I am beginning to understand things a bit more so I like it, especially because some of it helps me in my meditation. It's a little bit complicated sometimes but, in our tradition of Buddhism, it's really important to receive the 'transmission' of a text before you study it. This means the whole text is read to you, just as it was by your teacher's teacher to him, in a long line running all the way back to the enlightened master who originally wrote it. I suppose that even if I don't understand it all now, at least when I get a bit older I will be able to study it. Hopefully I will be able to understand it a bit more then!

Why I am a Buddhist

When people ask me why am I a Buddhist I suppose the first thing I say is it's because my parents are. Sometimes people kick off and say it's not right for them to push their religion on me but, if my parents didn't tell me about their religion I wouldn't know what it was! Now that I do know, I can make my own decision. I've thought about other religions and they just don't seem logical to me; I find it difficult to believe someone else is going to get rid of my problems. But Buddhism seems totally logical to me because it teaches me how to sort out my own problems myself.

B Here I am, receiving teachings from my lama.

I just think if I didn't believe in Buddhism, I wouldn't believe in anything at all, and I wouldn't be able to bear that. After all, what's the point in a life where you just do the same boring things every day until you die? You know: get born; go to school; get a job; retire; die. What's the point in that?

Today at school

School was pretty full on today: people were getting really wound up. Even though everyone else was getting like that, I was really pleased that I stayed calm. I find that because I am thinking about other people, I feel happier. When I do get angry, if I feel like criticising or hitting someone, something else in me reminds me that anything I do to other people will eventually happen to me; usually that stops me doing it!

If it looks like my mates are going to have a fight, I always try to talk them out of it and make them think about what will happen if they do. I mean, I can't talk about karma or future lives and stuff but, it seems to me, you don't have to wait until the next life to see how doing bad things makes you suffer; sometimes it only takes five minutes before you wish you hadn't done something!

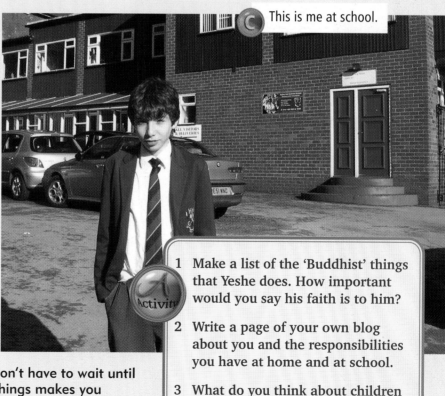
C This is me at school.

Activity

1 Make a list of the 'Buddhist' things that Yeshe does. How important would you say his faith is to him?

2 Write a page of your own blog about you and the responsibilities you have at home and at school.

3 What do you think about children following their parents' religion? Discuss the pros and cons with a partner and then feed back your views to the rest of the class.

The Buddhist sangha

objective

to understand how Buddhists with families and Buddhists who live in monasteries support each other

glossary

Bhikkhu
Enlightenment
Five Precepts
Sangha
Upasaka

Bhikkhus

Sangha

Upasakas

A

The community of people who practice Buddhism is called the **sangha**. There are two main groups in the sangha: those who live in monasteries and nunneries; and those who live an ordinary family life.

The Buddhist word for monk is **bhikkhu**: this means 'one who shares'. They are called this because whenever donations are given to a monastery, each bhikkhu is given a share to live on. Bhikkhus keep around 250 vows. The main aim of keeping these vows is to help focus the mind on achieving the Buddhist goals of escaping suffering and reaching **enlightenment**. One of the most important vows is not to have sex.

Activity

1 a Why do you think not having sex is one of the most important vows for Buddhist monks?

b Do you think it would be peaceful or painful to live as a monk or nun? Explain your answer.

c Imagine you have decided to become a monk or nun. Write a letter to your parents explaining why.

The Five Precepts

Buddhists who live an ordinary family life are called **upasakas**. Upasakas, Buddhists who are not monks or nuns, keep five vows, called the **Five Precepts (B)**.

1 Do not take life.
2 Do not steal.
3 Do not lie.
4 Do not have sex with someone else's partner.
5 Do not drink.

Buddhists believe that relationships are very important and that people being unfaithful is a major cause of suffering. That is why one of the Five Precepts is about sex and committed relationships. Also, Buddhists feel that alcohol only masks suffering when Buddhists should be facing up to reality, not hiding from it.

Activity

2 a Does deciding not to do things make you a better person? Why?

b Think of *five* precepts for your school. Design a poster explaining why students should keep them.

How upasakas and bhikkhus help each other

There has always been a strong link between the two kinds of sangha. Buddhists with families don't get much time to meditate. In Buddhist countries, upasakas get over this problem by supporting the bhikkhus. Giving to the monks is very good karma, helping the upasakas get a good rebirth.

Because the bhikkhus don't have to spend lots of time getting money for food, clothing and accommodation, they can spend lots of time studying and meditating. In return for their support, the bhikkhus give teachings to the upasakas and guide them on the Buddhist path. So, the upasakas provide the bhikkhus with their worldly needs and the bhikkhus provide the upasakas with their spiritual needs.

Activity

3 a Is there something that you really like doing or is really important to you? What gets in the way of you spending more time on it? Wouldn't it be good to find someone who was able to take these obstacles out of your way? Design an advert for this person, stressing the sort of jobs they'll be taking on and what you'd be able to help them with in return.

b Look at the photos in **A**, showing bhikkhus and upasakak. In your book or folder, write a speech bubble for each type of Buddhist to describe what they might say to each other.

c Draw a diagram to explain the partnership between bhikkhus and upasakas.

C Buddhist monks receiving alms from a lay Buddhist.

35

The Dechen Community

objective

to review how one Buddhist sangha (community) works to keep the Buddha's teaching alive in the West

glossary

Dharma
Guru

Since Buddhism first arrived in the West from Asia in the early 1900s, many of the different traditions have established groups here. One such group is the Dechen Community. Dechen is pronounced 'day-chen' and is a Tibetan word that means 'great bliss', something Tibetan Buddhists believe to be one of the results of practising meditation. The community was set up in the mid 1970s by a Tibetan lama called Karma Thinley Rinpoche with the help of his English student, Lama Jampa Thaye.

A A meditation class.

Each of Dechen's centres runs weekly meditation classes where beginners are taught the basics of the Buddhist path by experienced students. Once these beginners have some understanding of these basics, they are invited to attend teachings on more advanced topics.

After a time, some may even go on to receive instructions on the highest teachings from within Tibetan Buddhism from Rinpoche, Lama Jampa or other senior lamas. In this way, Westerners can receive a thorough education in the Tibetan form of Buddhism and learn to practice it in a traditional and gradual fashion, just as it was in the East for hundreds, indeed thousands, of years.

B A meditation poster.

The Sakya Buddhist Centre

Introductory Evenings - Tuesdays 8pm

...rville Road
Bristol BS6 5BX

0117 924 4424
bristol@dechen.org
www.dechen.org

C Westerners receiving instructions from Lama Jampa Thaye.

D Lama Jampa Thaye with H. H. Sakya Trizin, head of one of the four main schools of Tibetan Buddhism.

1 a Are brand names important to you? Which do you prefer: a famous brand of cola; or the supermarket version made to a similar recipe? Explain your choice.

b Do brand names matter in religion? What does the Dechen Community offer in its teachings that someone who had just read a lot of books about Buddhism could not?

c Why do you think Buddhists from other countries care how people in the UK learn about Buddhism? Think of *three* possible reasons.

Buddhism is still relevant today because people face the same basic problems as they did at the time of the Buddha.

E

No, I don't agree. We face many different problems today that the Buddha could never have thought of. Buddhism has to change with the times. I don't care if my Buddhism is very different from Buddhism in other countries – each to their own.

Buddhism in the West

In the eighth century, a Buddhist master called **Guru** Rinpoche made this prediction:

When the iron bird flies, and horses run on wheels, the Tibetan people will be scattered like ants across the world, and the **Dharma** will come to the land of the red faced people.

2 a The 'Dharma' is the Buddha's teaching. What do you think 'iron birds' that fly and horses that 'run on wheels' are, and who are the 'red faced people'?

b How do you explain the fact that someone could know about such things 1,200 years ago? How might a Buddhist explain this?

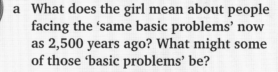

3 Read what the two people in E have to say about Buddhism in the West.

a What does the girl mean about people facing the 'same basic problems' now as 2,500 years ago? What might some of those 'basic problems' be?

b What might be some of the 'different problems' the boy is concerned about?

c If you decided to change Buddhist teachings to fit in with these 'different problems' would it still be right to call it 'Buddhism'?

Guru Rinpoche was certainly right that Buddhism would come to the West, and the contrast between a country like Tibet 1,200 years ago and a country like the UK could not really be greater! UK Buddhists feel Buddhism has a lot to offer people whatever century this is. But how can a religion that is thousands of years old do this? Does it need to change to fit the modern world?

Find out more about the activities of the Dechen Community by visiting their website. See www.nelsonthornes.com/religionsandbeliefs.

Teachings on society

objective

to consider some of the advice the Buddha gave on how to act towards other people in society

glossary

Social code

Our society is made up of lots of different people in different roles all working together. People usually think that Buddhism is only about changing your own 'inner world', your mind, rather than changing the world around you. In fact, as well as giving teachings on meditation, the Buddha also gave very precise advice on how people should behave towards one another. Buddhism encourages things like generosity, patience and non-violence. Some might even say that Buddhism is a complete **social code** which tells Buddhists how to interact with others.

Parents

The Buddha said this about parents:

> Having been supported by them, I will support them.

1 Do you think it is right for a religion to be involved in social affairs or should believers mind their own business? Make sure you have *two* reasons to back up your opinion before you share it with others.

2 a Write an advert for an old people's home. Your target is busy career couples whose elderly parents are becoming 'difficult to manage'. How would your advert persuade people to put their parents in your home?

   b Now ask yourself what you would like your children to do with you when you get old and 'difficult to manage'. Would you agree with the Buddha, or be happy with life in the old people's home?

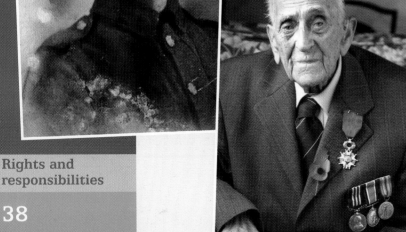

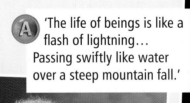

A 'The life of beings is like a flash of lightning... Passing swiftly like water over a steep mountain fall.'

Rights and responsibilities

Teachers

The Buddha taught that a good student should show respect by standing when their teacher enters the room, by paying attention, and by trying to learn what he or she has been taught.

> 3 What is a school for? How would you organise how teachers and students behave in your school and why?

The Buddha said that when someone is being taught, people should not just think about how they see their teacher; instead they should listen to the teacher's words. How might this advice help a Buddhist student who doesn't like a particular teacher?

Partner

According to the Buddha, a man should look after his partner by respecting and not criticising her; being faithful to her; giving her authority in the home; and giving her presents. A woman should look after her partner by doing her duties well; treating his family just like her own; being faithful; protecting the family's belongings; and by being clever and hard working.

> 4 A lot of things have changed since the Buddha's teaching. Women have fought to get more equality with men. So, is the Buddha's teaching out of date? Which parts of the teaching would you change, and in what way?

Friends

A good friend, according to the Buddha, should be helpful, respectful and caring through good times and bad. A good friend should speak kindly; lead others to do the right thing; be sympathetic; true to their word; and give gifts.

> 5 a Design an advert: 'Wanted: Good mates'. List the things you look for in a good friend.
>
>   b How many of the qualities you came up with are also on the Buddha's list?

Employees

The Buddha taught that employees should not be overworked; they should be paid and fed enough, and provided with health care.

> 6 2,500 years after the Buddha gave his advice, people still have to pay for their own health care in many parts of the world; in other parts of the world there may be no health care at all. Write a letter to the prime minister of such a country from the Buddha. What do you think the Buddha would say?

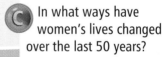

In what ways have women's lives changed over the last 50 years?

The tsunami disaster

objective

to see how Buddhist teachings on community responsibility were put into practice during the tsunami disaster at the end of 2004

glossary

Tsunami

On the morning of 26 December 2004, at 00:58 GMT, a massive earthquake under the sea off the coast of Sumatra, Indonesia, led to one of the biggest natural disasters humankind has ever seen. The energy released by the quake was estimated as being equal to 23,000 Hiroshima-sized atomic bombs. By the time it reached land, the resulting wave, or **tsunami**, was between four and 10 metres high.

All in all, the tsunami claimed the lives of nearly a quarter of a million people, one third of them children. Around five million people in 13 countries lost their homes, and tens of thousands of children lost their entire families. The estimated cost of aid and reconstruction was put at £6 billion.

People all over the world did all they could to help. Buddhists felt a particular connection because so many of the countries affected were Buddhist countries. This topic is about what one Buddhist community did to help.

The London Buddhist Vihara

As soon as they became aware of the scale of the disaster, monks and lay people at the London Buddhist Vihara, a Sri Lankan Buddhist temple in Chiswick, set up a relief fund for the victims of the disaster and made a public appeal for food, clothing, and medical supplies. Over the following weeks, a huge army of volunteers worked together to sort and pack donated supplies before shipping them out to Sri Lanka.

Ⓐ Boxes of donations at the London Buddhist Vihara.

HRH Prince Charles

On 10 January 2005, Prince Charles visited the centre where he made offerings at a shrine to the Buddha and met the many volunteers who were co-ordinating the aid effort. As well as praising them for their work, Prince Charles made a big donation to the fund and even helped personally to arrange for the dispatch of a large quantity of medical supplies to the region.

During his speech, the Prince said:

We hear a certain amount about how, as a result of this terrible disaster, people's faith might be challenged, and it is very easy to understand how that might happen. Nevertheless, I think it has also helped in a strange way to reveal the love and compassion that exists in people's hearts, otherwise we would not have had this remarkable reaction.

1 People around the world gave huge amounts of money to help the victims of the tsunami. Just a week after the tsunami, Britain had raised £189 million, Germany had raised £200 million and Australia £88 million. In fact, people raised more money than their governments were giving!

  a How would a Buddhist explain what Prince Charles called 'this remarkable reaction'?

  b How might a Buddhist affected by the tsunami use the Buddha's teachings to help him or her
    i) understand and
    ii) deal with the results of the disaster?

  c Do you think some people gave up being Buddhists after the tsunami disaster? Explain your answer.

Medium and long-term projects

By the end of March 2005, as well as sending medicines, wheelchairs and 80,000 kilos of food, the Vihara had also managed to raise just under £68,000 to help finance medium and long-term projects. These included paying for rebuilding in those areas where housing had been destroyed and setting up 'twinning' programs between UK and Sri Lankan schools. Some of the money was also given to groups like IMPAKT Aid, charities that had been set up in Sri Lanka itself as a result of the disaster.

To find out more about the London Buddhist Vihara's charitable activities in Sri Lanka and IMPAKT Aid's work, visit their websites. See www.nelsonthornes.com/religionsandbeliefs.

2 Imagine there has been another disaster in the world: an enormous earthquake in a remote, mountainous country during winter. Many people in your neighbourhood have relatives in the affected country. You and three or four other students work for a Buddhist charity here in the UK. Your job is now to decide:

  a what kind of things the victims of the disaster need

  b how you are going to raise funds and send supplies to them

  c what kind of spiritual help you can provide in your community for those worried about their relatives

  d what message to use in your fundraising adverts. These will go out into the Buddhist community and should explain why Buddhists need to help.

Each group should then present details of its programme to the rest of the class. Finally, vote on which of the programmes you feel would be the most effective, giving reasons for your decision.

B HRH Prince Charles arriving at the London Buddhist Vihara.

Assessment for Unit 2

The great Buddhist master Padmasambhava, or 'Guru Rinpoche', whom Tibetans refer to as 'the Second Buddha', was the main force behind establishing Buddhism in Tibet in the eighth century. Padmasambhava famously said:

'Though my view is like the sky, my actions are like grains of sand.'

In other words, even though Buddhism is a religion that stresses the importance of realising the 'space' of no self, it is equally important that those who wish to understand that space are very careful about all of their actions, no matter how small or unimportant they might seem. A good Buddhist, then, is not some kind of 'space case'; rather he or she always tries to follow the practical advice the Buddha gave on how to act in all situations.

These questions test different sets of skills in RE. Which skills do you need to work on? Choose the level you need and work through the tasks set.

Level 3

- Design a poster that explains the ten negative actions.
- Even though we might not be religious, many of the rules we live our lives by are similar to religious ones. Make a list of your own 'life rules'; then say which rules are also religious ones.
- Make *two* spider diagrams to show what kind of things might happen in:
  a) 'a world without rules'
  b) 'a world with rules'.

Level 4

- Explain how Buddhists in a relationship should treat one another.
- A Buddhist would say that one of the most important things in a relationship is love. What do they mean by this? In what way is this love different from the one many people mean when they say 'I love you'?
- Some people say 'always look after number one', while others say 'always put others first'. List some advantages and disadvantages of each attitude. Now say which approach to life you think is best and why.

Level 5

- Explain the advice that the Buddha gave people on how to relate to different members of their community.
- List the different Buddhist beliefs that might cause people to help when a huge natural disaster occurs. With each belief, explain the thinking behind the decision to help.
- Recently, there have been a number of natural disasters that have led to charities making worldwide appeals for help. Did you offer any help? Why/why not?

Level 6

- Create a wall chart to explain the Noble Eightfold Path.
- List some of the difficulties a Buddhist might face following the Noble Eightfold Path in today's busy world.
- You have just been introduced to a Buddhist who has been following the Noble Eightfold Path for many years. Write a letter to a friend explaining what the person was like.

We're not on our own!

Wealth and poverty

objective

to understand what Buddhists mean by the 'middle way' and to work through Buddhist views on wealth and poverty

glossary

Buddha
Craving
Enlightenment
Karma
Middle way
Rebirth

The life of the **Buddha** shows a lot about Buddhist attitudes to wealth and poverty – having lots of money or having none. The Buddha passed the first part of his life as a young prince surrounded by wealth and possessions, but eventually chose to leave his privileged lifestyle behind and, instead, become a wandering beggar.

The young Buddha-to-be (Siddhartha Gotama) clearly felt that, no matter how much wealth he had, no matter how many things he owned, none of them could bring him true, lasting happiness. So, for Buddhists, wealth does not equal happiness.

> 1 Write a letter from the young prince, Siddhartha Gotama, to his father, explaining why he is leaving the palace.
>
> Activity

The second important stage in the Buddha's life began with him giving up lots of things and living a life of extreme hardship, sometimes eating only a single grain of rice a day for food. By the end of six years, he realised that he was getting closer to death than to **enlightenment**, and he decided that poverty does not equal happiness either.

Middle way

Self-indulgence   Self-denial

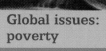
B

The middle way

The Buddha-to-be realised that achieving real happiness didn't depend on having great wealth or living in extreme poverty. What he said was that the way to freedom was to live a life that was a '**middle way**' between the two lifestyles of self-indulgence and self-denial.

For Buddhists, both wealth and poverty are the result of former actions, or **karma**. Wealth is the result of giving in previous lives and poverty is the result of greed and miserliness in previous lives. Thinking like this helps Buddhists feel more relaxed and accepting when they experience either wealth or poverty in their lives.

Buddhists do not believe that all wealth or the desire for wealth is bad. Whether it is bad or not is determined by how you get it. Working to generate wealth is perfectly acceptable for a Buddhist layperson as long as it does not involve 'wrong livelihoods' (see page 27) such as trading in meat or weapons.

> 2 Can you think of any other jobs that Buddhists might think are wrong? What about the jobs shown in pictures **C–E**? Would these be right livelihoods?
>
> Activity

A The Buddha realised from personal experience that poverty does not equal happiness.

Craving

While they do not consider all wealth to be bad, Buddhists do believe that **craving** for wealth is suffering. For them, happiness and satisfaction come from not wanting more, rather than through making money and buying possessions. Not only does craving for wealth and possessions cause unhappiness and feelings of poverty in this life, it also causes **rebirth** as a hungry ghost after that. So craving for wealth is suffering in both the present and the future life.

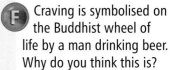

3 'Making money and buying things is not happiness.' Do you agree or disagree with this statement? Why?

As well as how you get it, wealth is also seen as good or bad depending on what you do with it. If you use it to buy poison or to spend just to impress people and make yourself look big, then it would be bad. If you use it to support a monk or your family, it would be good.

F Craving is symbolised on the Buddhist wheel of life by a man drinking beer. Why do you think this is?

Giving

The practice of giving is very important in all the main Buddhist traditions and many Buddhist ceremonies begin with an act of offering. Giving is believed to create good karma. In a Buddhist story, a famous Buddhist called Nagarjuna advises a king to use his wealth to, amongst other things, provide food and drink for the poor and needy, as well as free medical care, cheap goods and low taxes!

G Nagarjuna.

C Working in a cigarette factory.

D Politician.

E Veterinary surgeon.

The Buddha said:

The fool ruins himself through craving for riches.

4 a What would you have advised the king to spend his money on if you were Nagarjuna?

b Modern life often seems to be all about the desire for wealth and possessions. And, yet, Buddhism is more and more popular in the West. How would you explain these two contradictory things?

c Complete a copy of table **H**, outlining Buddhist attitudes to wealth and poverty. Explain your own attitudes towards the subject and then comment on similarities and differences.

Buddhist views	My views	Similarities	Differences
Wealth and poverty			

H

The Nuns of Tekchen Lekshay Ling

objective

to consider the ways Buddhists in the rich West support nuns who own nothing in India and Nepal, and to reflect on Buddhist teachings on wealth and poverty

glossary

Meditation
Scriptures

Over the last 30 years, growing numbers of Tibetan Buddhist nuns have left their homeland to live in safety in India and Nepal. Since the 1950s, Tibet has been occupied by Chinese forces, which has made it very difficult for Buddhist monks and nuns to continue their traditions in their own country. Many monks and nuns who have escaped, report suffering torture and imprisonment. Some spent two years walking though the Himalayan Mountains to reach a land where they knew they would be free to practice their religion.

1 Imagine you are a Buddhist monk or nun living in a country where your religion has been made illegal. Write a letter to a friend overseas explaining the difficulties you are experiencing and how it makes you feel.

Tekchen Lekshay Ling, a Buddhist temple in Boudhanath, Nepal, is home to a group of 21 nuns, many of whom have endured such hardships. This is the most important place of Buddhist pilgrimage in the Himalayas as it contains the remains of an ancient Buddha.

A day in the life of a Lekshay Ling nun

The nuns spend many hours each day meditating and praying. **A** shows a timetable for an average day.

A

4:30–6.30 am:	prayer and meditation.
6.30–8.00 am:	breakfast and break; breakfast is usually Tibetan tea (made with salt and butter instead of sugar), and a tennis ball-sized lump of dough called 'Tsampa', roasted barley flour mixed with tea.
8:00–11:30 am:	having eaten breakfast, the nuns continue to pray.
11:30 am:	lunch and break; lunch is normally rice, vegetables and dumplings. After lunch, the nuns rest.
1.30–3.00 pm:	personal prayers and memorising Buddhist **scriptures**.
3.00–5.00 pm:	nuns join together to pray to the Buddha to bless and protect themselves and all beings.
5.00–6.30 pm:	break for soup and tea.
6.30–7.30 pm:	prayer or teaching.
9.00 pm:	bedtime/personal prayer time.

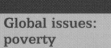

A Buddhist prayer:
I go for refuge to the Buddha, Dharma, and Sangha,
From now until enlightenment.
By the merit I create from the practice of giving and other perfections
May I become a Buddha, in order to benefit all beings.

Donations

The nuns have no possessions; they don't own houses or get paid a wage. They are as poor as anyone can be because they have given up everything to devote themselves to Buddhism. How do they afford to eat, get clothes or be looked after when they are ill?

The Lekshay Ling nuns are able to do this because of the financial help they receive from the Dechen Community, a group of European Tibetan Buddhists based in the UK (see pages 36–37). In 2004, around 70% of the money raised from the voluntary donations made to the Community went to support Lekshay Ling. As well as helping to pay for the nuns' daily needs, the money was also used to pay for the building of a 'retreat' centre where the nuns can completely withdraw from the outside world and practice **meditation** in total seclusion, sometimes for as long as three years at a time!

2 A nun's life at Lekshay Ling is long and demanding. What questions would you like to ask a nun from this place? In groups, put together your questions and then meet as a class to discuss which *five* questions you would most like to send. Then e-mail them to buddhism@nelsonthornes.com for your answers.

3 Why would UK Buddhists think that building this retreat was a good use of their money?

Giving is a very good action for Buddhists, especially giving to help a monk or nun. So the UK Buddhists believe that helping the nuns will bring them happiness in future lives – because they helped the nuns, others will help them in turn. The nuns try to repay the kindness of those who support them by constantly making prayers for them.

The thing about supporting the nuns is that, most of us here in the West don't have the opportunity to practise so intensively. Supporting the nuns gives us the chance to share in the incredible good karma that these women are creating while, at the same time, doing something good for a fellow human being!

Dechen Community member

4 a The nuns at Lekshay Ling are very poor and many have had very hard lives. What present would you like to buy or make them to make their lives more comfortable? Money is no object: buy whatever you like.

b Your present has been received and the nuns have written back to you. Write the letter you think they would send.

47

Buddhism and animal rights

objective

to learn what Buddhists believe about how humans should treat animals

glossary

Five Precepts
Vegetarian
Vinaya

Buddhists believe they should try not to harm any living beings. This rule is one of the **Five Precepts** (see pages 34–35). It is why Buddhists are against conflict with people. Doing any harm to another person, even if it is only saying something nasty about them behind their back, is a negative action: bad karma.

Not harming others applies to animals too, so harming or killing any animal is to be avoided. Some Buddhists are **vegetarians** because of this. One scripture, called The Descent into Lanka Sutra, lists a number of reasons why it is wrong for Buddhists to eat meat, including:

- all beings have been our relatives in previous lives
- meat production involves killing
- meat eating causes rebirth as a meat-eater
- those who eat meat cannot make progress in meditation.

> 1 'Those who eat meat cannot make progress in meditation.' Why might some Buddhists think this?
>
> Activity

However not all Buddhists are vegetarians. An important Buddhist scripture, called the **Vinaya**, says that it is wrong to eat meat that has been killed especially for you. This would involve you in the killing of the animal and, as a result, you will eventually experience bad karma. But if you are not involved in the killing of the animal, the Vinaya says it is perfectly acceptable to eat its meat.

A How much suffering happened to create this display?

English farmhouse veal topside animals reared in small groups in barns with straw bedding £22.99 kg £10.43 lb

Aberdeen Angus bone in prime rib of beef £8.99 £4.08

> 2 Does regularly buying meat at a supermarket involve you in the killing of animals? Think of your argument and reasons. Debate the question and then vote on it.
>
> Activity

A Tibetan Buddhist was asked why he was not a vegetarian. 'How many animals must die for me to eat a piece of meat?' the Buddhist asked. 'One,' came the reply. 'And how many animals must die for me to be able to eat cabbage?'

What was this Buddhist saying? Look at photo **B** as well as the following text. Do you agree with him?

B

Modern agriculture depends on chemicals to get rid of insect pests. Getting rid of insects affects the animals and birds that would have eaten them. Fewer of these animals being around means less to eat for predators – foxes, owls, stoats, hawks, etc. So do cabbages cost lives?

Animal experimentation

Large-scale animal experimentation is only a recent development. Because of this, Buddhist scripture has nothing to say about it specifically. However, because Buddhists consider it wrong to kill or harm others, many present-day Buddhists feel it is totally wrong to use animals in experiments.

Other Buddhists think that animal experimentation is acceptable but only under certain circumstances. They say that if, through the suffering of a small number of beings, the lives of a greater number could be saved, then such experiments are acceptable.

Medical research

One area where some Buddhists might consider experimentation acceptable is in the field of medical research; many steps forward in the fight against disease have been made as a result of such experiments. Nowadays, large drug companies in Japan often pay for annual Buddhist memorial ceremonies for beings harmed during research.

3 a If UK animal experimentation companies did something here to commemorate the animals who had suffered in order that humans could cure diseases, would that be seen as a good or a bad thing? Maybe some people would think they were barking mad! What do you think? Explain your answer.

   b Rebirth as a human is seen as a very precious opportunity in Buddhism. Does this mean that human life and human suffering are more important than animal life and animal suffering for Buddhists? Write down your thoughts.

Product testing

While some Buddhists might accept animal experimentation in the name of medicine, it is almost certain that none would accept the use of animals in the development of cosmetics.

C If these experiments produced a drug which could cure the person in the picture, would the experiment be acceptable?

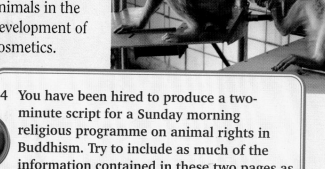

D Photos like these caused a massive explosion in the demand for products that had not been tested on animals. Why do you think it took people in this country so long to object to animal testing in cosmetics?

4 You have been hired to produce a two-minute script for a Sunday morning religious programme on animal rights in Buddhism. Try to include as much of the information contained in these two pages as you can. Make karma and not harming others the central themes of your script.

The Monkey King

objective

to unpick some of
the meanings about
how humans
should treat
animals in a
Buddhist story

*This story comes from the Jataka Tales, a
collection of 547 stories about the previous
lives of the Buddha. Each of them shows the
kind of qualities a person needs to develop if
they want to reach enlightenment. The
Monkey King story looks at the relationship
between humans and animals.*

At one time, in a life before he became
Buddha, Siddhartha Gotama was born as the
king of a troop of monkeys who lived high in
the Himalayan Mountains. There, on the
edge of a gorge cut by the mighty River
Ganga, the king lived with his subjects in a
huge and exotic fruit tree.

Because the fruits of this tree were so
delicious, the animals were always worried.
They knew that if the fruit were to fall into
the river below it would be carried down to
the cities of men. If men were to taste it, all
of the animals knew they would come
looking for the tree it came from; they all
knew that this could only spell disaster. So,
the monkeys were given the important job of
making sure that this didn't happen. As soon
as the fruits ripened, they would pluck the
fruits and share them between all of the
animals of the forest.

One day, a fruit accidentally dropped
into the river and sure enough, later
that same day, a fisherman sat on the
riverbank saw the fruit floating by.
Never having seen such a fruit before,
he plucked it from the river and
rushed to the royal palace with it,
hoping to receive a reward for his
rare prize.

As soon as the king tasted the fruit he
felt he could never be happy until he
found the tree that bore it. He
immediately gathered his troops and
set off towards the mountains, in
search of the tree.

A monkey lookout saw the king and his approaching army in the distance but, before they could make their escape, the tree was completely surrounded. Peering across to the other side of the mighty gorge, the Monkey King spied a tree. Realising that if he could make some kind of bridge to the tree, he would be able to free his subjects, he gathered together all of his strength and, in one mighty bound, leapt the gorge. Once across, he tied one end of a long piece of elephant grass around the tree, the other, around his ankle and then leapt back to complete the bridge.

Sadly, the Monkey King had misjudged the distance: although he was able to reach the fruit tree, he was only just able to hold on to it. Even though his body was in great pain, he ordered his subjects to climb along his body and the elephant grass to freedom.

One by one they clambered across but, as the final monkey made his way to safety, the Monkey King's back broke under the strain. His body crashed down on to the rocks below.

The dying monkey was brought before the human king. 'Why did you put yourself in danger for them? Why have you given your life like this?'

'They have always loved me,' replied the Monkey King. 'I too loved them and do not suffer in leaving this world because I know I have helped them. More than that,' he continued, 'If my death shows you that a true king rules by love and not by the sword, then I can die without regret.' Then, holding the king's hand, he died.

His eyes filled with tears, the king vowed never to return to disturb the animals and, from then on, he ruled with a kind and loving heart.

Activity

1 Retell the story of Monkey King in words, pictures, or as a drama.

2 Religious stories have messages in them that teach people things. What do you think this story's message is? Who is the hero of the story?

3 Based on the Monkey King story, what would you say were the Buddhist attitudes towards:

   a how humans treat other living beings

   b how humans should treat other living beings?

   Give evidence to back up your answer.

4 What qualities do you think we can learn from animals? Design a series of posters for display around schools or offices that use pictures of animals to inspire people to: be more patient with others; be more positive about their work; work well as a team; relax; and have fun.

Protecting the environment

objective

to understand Buddhist attitudes towards environmental issues, and to learn about engaged Buddhism

glossary

Compassion
Desire
Engaged Buddhist
Non-sentient
Reforestation
Sentient

Most people in this country have heard about environmental issues. Scientists have shown that humans are having a major impact on the world around us: poisoning rivers and seas with chemicals; polluting the atmosphere with fumes and gases; destroying forests; and even changing climates around the world.

Buddhist scriptures do not talk much about environmental issues: environmental problems like the ones we have nowadays were not an issue for early Buddhists. However, even today some Buddhists might not see the issues surrounding the natural environment as very important in themselves.

Sentient or non-sentient

One reason for this might be because of the way Buddhists divide the universe and its contents into '**sentient**' beings that can think, feel, and suffer and '**non-sentient**' forms that can't – objects like buildings, cars, and so on. For the majority of Buddhists, plants and rocks are usually seen as non-sentient. For Buddhists, the main focus of their religion is sentient beings.

1 Look at the four pictures in **A**. Which ones would a Buddhist describe as sentient, and which as non-sentient?

Nevertheless, early writings show that the Buddha himself always tried to avoid harming plants. Burning trees and woodlands was forbidden in some scriptures, and (some) monks had rules against damaging plants and vegetables and cutting down trees. The Buddhist emperor Asoka (268–239 BCE) outlawed the burning of forests unless there was a good reason. But none of this was really to protect the plants and trees of the natural environment.

Buddhists protect the environment for another reason: because of **compassion** towards sentient beings living in and around plants and trees. This includes animals and insects, but also gods and spirits. It is a commonly held belief in Buddhist cultures that some trees are 'mansions' of the gods; other beings live in healing herbs, and others in rocks or on the land. Even in modern Thailand, when Thai people build on previously unused land, they build miniature houses to accommodate the spirits that live on that land. Tibetan Buddhists also always make offerings to local gods and spirits before they start building projects. So, the main reason a Buddhist shows concern for the environment is out of concern for the beings in that environment and not the environment itself.

Who's to blame?

Some present-day Buddhists blame 'Western values' for environmental problems. They say that the Western idea that happiness comes from owning more and more 'things' – cars, clothes, 'consumables' that get thrown away as soon as they are out of fashion – will lead to the material world getting used up, and that humans' **desire** to conquer nature will eventually destroy it. They believe that Buddhist ideas like concern for others should also cover the environment.

Some modern-day Buddhists feel they should become actively involved in protecting the environment. These socially-active Buddhists are known as '**engaged Buddhists**' because, using Buddhist thinking, they engage in action to deal with social problems.

Engaged Buddhism has had a big impact on Buddhists in Asian countries like Cambodia, Thailand and Sri Lanka. In Thailand, for instance, monks now run advice courses for villagers on the preservation of nature. Elsewhere, monasteries have bought land for **reforestation** and even tried to stop a dam being built by going to live in the flood zone!

2 a Some property developers have applied to the city council for permission to build a factory at a local beauty spot. Write a letter of protest to a local paper, using Buddhist arguments.

b Some Buddhists think that 'engaged Buddhism' isn't really Buddhism at all, because the Buddha's main concern was preventing the suffering that beings experienced. Do you agree or disagree? Explain why.

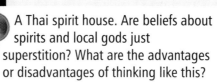

B A Thai spirit house. Are beliefs about spirits and local gods just superstition? What are the advantages or disadvantages of thinking like this?

The forest monk

In the forested hills of Northern Thailand, forest tribes have recently taken up 'slash and burn' agriculture to create land on which they can grow crops. This type of agriculture is causing **deforestation**.

A Is this progress?

1 It is said that deforestation have long-term consequenc for the whole planet, but w do you think the short-term consequences for those bei who live in and around the Thai forest will be?

Activity

Ajahn Tejadhammo

In the 1970s, an Australian-born Buddhist monk of the Theravada tradition called Ajahn Tejadhammo was living in those same hills. He saw a tobacco company move into the lowland forests and start destroying them; local villagers finished the trees off. At the same time, hill tribes moved into the highland forests and started to clear the forests for crops.

B Ajahn Tejadham

The consequences of this were terrible for both the forest environment and the beings who lived in it. Because of the destruction of trees in the highlands, the soil could no longer hold water and much of it was being carried away; the highlands were becoming more like desert than forest.

In the lowlands, forest loss meant that streams that many relied upon would suddenly dry up or change course, sometimes with disastrous consequences for people living near them.

In the early 1980s, Ajahn Tejadhammo began to organise the people of one forest valley, arranging schemes to protect and rebuild the forest in a way that would provide villagers with food and a livelihood.

Maintaining the balance of nature

Ajahn Tejadhammo stresses the importance of maintaining the balance of nature, which he says is damaged by people not behaving properly, and not being careful about their effect on the environment. To correct this, his followers work in the forest, conserving and rebuilding natural resources, and in the community through development programmes that encourage people to be environmentally friendly. They try to teach villagers to recognise that everyone and everything in the universe is interconnected.

Ajahn Tejadhammo says that, because the forest provides them with everything, villagers have a duty to protect it and be grateful to it. The forest is spoken of as a second parent and the animals are seen as the villagers' brothers and sisters.

2   a   How do the consequences of deforestation fit in with the Buddhist idea that everything is interconnected?

b   Why is the forest like a second parent for these people?

c   Why would a Buddhist say the animals are like brothers and sisters?

The word spread

By 1985, 274 villages were involved. Ajahn Tejadhammo and his followers had replanted half a square kilometre and had plans to replant a further eight. Because of their work, many villagers became involved in canal and reservoir building, planting thousands and thousands of seedlings; they ran tree nurseries and helped rebuild crumbling hillsides. By 1992, over 97,000 people in 1,000 villages were involved!

Ajahn Tejadhammo's contribution to protecting the environment and those who live in it was recognised in 1990 when he was included in the UN Environmental Programme's 'Global 500 Role of Honour'.

The 'monk tree' story

However, Ajahn Tejadhammo does not just preach Buddhism and conservation. He believes it is his Buddhist duty to become actively involved in political protest against environmental damage. In 1990, his followers camped out in an ancient forest that was about to be flooded by the building of a dam. In 1991, in the north-east of Thailand, one monk even began ordaining trees as Buddhist monks so that people would be too afraid to cut them down.

3   a   You are a TV reporter. Plan an interview about the 'monk tree' story. What questions would you ask the monks? Journalists often plan their questions around the five Ws: Who? Where? What? When? and Why?

b   What does the fact that a 'forest monk' has become so politically active tell you about what he thinks the duties of a Buddhist are?

c   Are these people going too far? Should Buddhists just keep themselves to themselves?

d   'In 1945, 70% of Thailand was covered in natural forest; in 1989 only 15% was covered.' Ajahn Tejadhammo is only one person. Is there any real point to his work? Explain your answer.

Buddhism and war

Many world leaders today seem to think that the way to end conflict is to go to war. You might explain this theory like a maths sum (**A**).

1 Explain the meaning of the last two sums in **A** and say why you agree or disagree with them. Share your views with others, peacefully!

A

aggression + aggression = peace.

The Buddhist view couldn't be more different. The Buddhist sum would be:

aggression + aggression = aggression x 2

and that:

aggression + patience = aggression ÷ 2

B What is this young person trying to say to the soldiers?

2 For a minute, think what the Buddha meant by this quote opposite and then write down your thoughts, putting the quote in your own words.

The Buddha said that:

Hatred is never brought to an end by hatred in this world. Only by a lack of hatred is it brought to an end.

Karma: What goes around, comes around

Because Buddhists believe in karma (the idea that the things you do to others in this life will happen to you in a later life), they say no one can ever really win a war. The Buddha told two warring kings:

The conqueror gets a conqueror...

In other words, those who win wars in one life will be the losers in a later life. Therefore, for Buddhists, what people call 'victory' is only really a break in the fighting. Over the course of many lifetimes, everyone who wins a fight will also lose a fight. Long term, it is impossible to stop fighting by fighting.

3 Draw a spider diagram with 'Why war?' in the middle. Now write around it all the reasons you have heard of for why we have wars. Which reasons do you think make good sense? Would a Buddhist agree with any of them?

The antidote to war

One way that Buddhists try to stop themselves getting angry with people who are angry at them is by seeing this anger as a result of something they did in a past life: their karma. A Buddhist master called Shantideva taught that when faced with anger, Buddhists should think:

> In the past I must have caused similar harm to other beings.
> Therefore it is only right for this harm to be returned
> To me, the cause of (past) injury to others.

In other words, rather than blaming the 'enemy' for their suffering, Buddhists try to blame their own past actions. Looking at it this way, what would be the point of fighting back – it would only create more problems for yourself in the future!

4 a Do you agree with the Buddhists about not fighting back? Give an example to back up your answer.

b What might a Buddhist head teacher do or say about bullying in your school? What would he say to the bullies? What would he say to the victims?

The real cause of war – 'us' and 'them'

For Buddhists, the sufferings of war happen because people always think of 'me' as being more important than 'you', of 'us' being better than 'them'. The Buddha taught that actually there is no 'me' and 'you'. So another way Buddhists say we could stop wars is by remembering that we are all the same and no one is more important than anyone else.

The Dalai Lama, a Tibetan Buddhist leader, said:

> Human beings are all basically the same; we are all made of flesh, bones and blood. Our inner feelings – our hopes, desires and ambitions – are all the same; we all want to be free from suffering and to find happiness, and we all have an equal right to be happy. Therefore, we belong to one big human family, which includes all the human beings on this planet.

5 a Draw an anti-war poster which uses the idea that we are all one big human family.

b Write a letter as a Buddhist to a politician explaining why war achieves nothing. You could also write the politician's reply.

C In what ways are you different from these children? In what ways are you the same?

The invasion of Tibet

objective

to learn about the invasion of Tibet and consider the Dalai Lama's message of non-violence

glossary

Lama

1 From what you know about Buddhism, why do you think the monks were looking for a child?

Activity

In 1937, a party of Tibetan monks set out from their country's capital, Lhasa. The old Dalai Lama, the Thirteenth, had been dead for four years and they were in search of their new leader. The Dalai Lamas were for centuries the political and religious leaders of Tibet and were recognised by Tibetans as living Buddhas. Yet, the monks weren't just looking for a great teacher or a successful politician to be their new leader. They were looking for a young child.

Lhamo Dhondup

Disguised as merchants, the monks arrived at the home of two year-old Lhamo Dhondup, a headstrong child who spoke with a Lhasa accent, although he had never been to the city (like finding a two year-old from Birmingham with a cockney accent)! As soon as Lhamo saw the 'merchants' seated in the kitchen, he took hold of the rosary around the neck of one of their servants and said, 'This is mine'. The servant was actually the abbot of a monastery called Sera. He told Lhamo he could have the beads if he could tell him who he really was. 'You are a **lama** from Sera,' replied Lhamo. Saying nothing, the party returned to Lhasa the following day. Lhamo sobbed as the travellers left, but they promised to return to see him again.

A The young fourteenth Dalai Lama (top) and the old thirteenth Dalai Lama (middle).

When they returned, the party brought with them a number of the old Dalai Lama's possessions along with some copies. Each time he was asked which was his, Lhamo identified the one that had belonged to the previous Dalai Lama. All of the party were convinced that the child was Tibet's fourteenth Dalai Lama.

Lhamo was ordained as a Buddhist monk and given the name Tenzin Gyatso. The young Dalai Lama received a thorough Buddhist education. However, a change of government in neighbouring China was about to drastically alter the course of his life and those of all of his subjects.

The invasion of Tibet

The Chinese communists declared: 'The task for the People's Liberation Army in 1950 is to liberate Tibet.' They claimed that Westerners were trying to take Tibet over and make it part of their empire. In reality, it seems there were only five Westerners in the whole of Tibet at the time. On the morning of 7 October 1950 the Chinese army invaded. The Tibetan army, heavily outnumbered and armed with antique weapons, was immediately destroyed. By March 1959, after having repeatedly tried to negotiate peace, and as concerns for his own safety grew, the Dalai Lama decided to leave Tibet. Two days later, not realising he was gone, the Chinese attacked his summer palace. By nightfall, the streets of Lhasa city were strewn with the bodies of more than 10,000 dead Tibetans.

It is thought that since 1950, 1.2 million Tibetans, almost a quarter of the country's population, have been killed. More than 6,000 religious buildings have been destroyed. A large number of Chinese people have settled in the country and Tibetans are now a poor minority in their own country. Even to the present day, there are reports that monks and nuns have been tortured and beaten for publicly praising the Dalai Lama. Amnesty International has reported that over 100 monks and nuns are in prison.

The Dalai Lama receives the Nobel Peace Prize

While many might respond with anger, the Dalai Lama has repeatedly stated that anger is a sign of weakness and that Tibetans will only be able to return to Tibet if they are patient, non-violent and compassionate towards their occupiers. In 1989, this approach led to him being awarded the Nobel Peace Prize. In his acceptance speech, the Dalai Lama said:

> Because violence can only breed more violence and suffering, our struggle must remain non-violent and free of hatred. We are trying to end the suffering of our people, not to inflict suffering upon others.

Activity

2 What sort of problems might you face if you always tried to be patient and non-violent? Make up a diary entry for a day when you took this approach.

3 Explain why, as a Buddhist, the Dalai Lama does not want the Tibetans to fight against the Chinese. Use the information on pages 26–27 and 56-57 in your answer.

4 Write a short outline for a film of the Dalai Lama's life. What would make people want to come and see your film?

5 In other countries that are occupied like Tibet, there is often a lot of violence to try and force the occupiers out. In fact in 1959 the Tibetans, after many years of attempts at a peaceful negotiation, did rise up against the Chinese. Their uprising was brutally crushed. Which approach – violent or non-violent – would you support?

6 The Chinese leader Mao told the Dalai Lama that 'religion is poison'. What did he mean? Do you agree? Why?

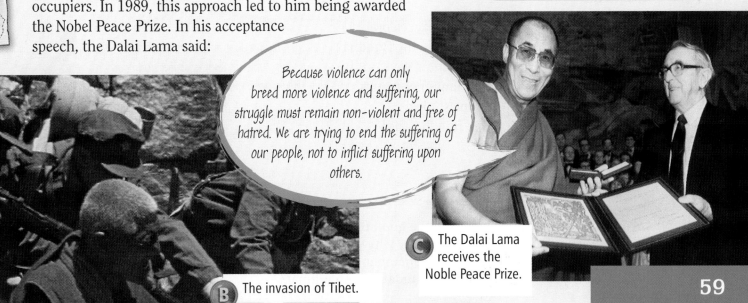

B The invasion of Tibet.

C The Dalai Lama receives the Noble Peace Prize.

Angulimala

This book has featured quite a bit of information about different Buddhist traditions. Although some of the traditions are very different from one another, in general there isn't the conflict between traditions that has so damaged the image of other religious traditions – between Catholic and Protestant Christians in Northern Ireland, for example, or Sunni and Shia Muslims in Iraq. This topic is about an organisation that brings together Buddhists from different traditions in this country.

In 1971, a young English actor with a promising career decided to leave it all behind and travel to Thailand to increase his understanding of Buddhism. Having been accepted as a student by one of Thailand's greatest meditation masters, the late Ajahn Chah, the young man ordained as a Buddhist monk or **bhikkhu** and received the name Khemadhammo Bhikkhu. Khemadhammo Bhikkhu spent the next six years studying and meditating in monasteries and forest hermitages throughout the north-east of Thailand.

In 1977, Khemadhammo Bhikkhu travelled back to England with his teacher Ajahn Chah. While staying in London, he was asked to visit Buddhist prisoners at Parkhurst, Pentonville, and Holloway prisons. Ajahn Chah asked Khemadhammo Bhikkhu to stay and he has been visiting prisons ever since. Nowadays, like his master before him, he is known as Ajahn Khemadhammo.

In 1985 on the day of Magha Puja, a Buddhist festival, Ajahn Khemadhammo set up an organisation called Angulimala. He wanted to provide Buddhist 'chaplains' for prisons throughout the UK. Soon after it was founded, Angulimala was recognised by the Prison Service in England and Wales as its official consultant on all things Buddhist.

Magha Puja celebrates an occasion in the Buddha's life when he gave out his teaching in one of its simplest forms. The Buddha said:

> *Give up what is unwholesome and wrong, cultivate what is skilful and good; Purify your mind – this is the teaching of the Buddha.*

objective

to see how Buddhists from different traditions work together to provide Buddhist teachings for people in prison

glossary

Bhikkhu
Nirvana

1 Giving up a job to go and find out more about a religion is a pretty big decision. How do you think Ajahn Khemadhammo came to that decision? Write an e-mail that he could have sent to his friends explaining what he had decided to do.

2 Read the quotation from the Buddha above. Say why you think Ajahn Khemadhammo chose this particular festival to launch Angulimala.

Angulimala was a mass murderer at the time of the Buddha, who cut off his victim's fingers and made a necklace from them; the name means 'necklace of fingers'. Later in life, Angulimala felt terrible regret for his actions and, after becoming a disciple of the Buddha, he reached **nirvana**.

What is special about Angulimala is the way in which it relies on nearly all of the different types of UK Buddhists to help provide its service for prisoners. While the organisation itself is led by a member of the Thai tradition, the chaplains can just as easily be followers of the Tibetan or Japanese Buddhist traditions.

> 3 What do you think the message of the story of Angulimala might be?

Angulimala holds four workshops a year for the followers of those different traditions who have been appointed Angulimala 'chaplains'. Meetings begin with meditation and continue with advice on how prisons are run, as well as how to offer Buddhist teaching and practice in this special and unusual environment.

A Ajahn Khemadhammo.

Angulimala has more than 50 Buddhist chaplains working in around 120 prisons throughout England and Wales. These are chaplains to the Buddhist inmates and anyone else who may be curious or interested. They may give talks on Buddhism, as well as advice on meditation and dealing with problems. They supply inmates with books, Buddha images and pictures and prisoners sometimes set up shrines in their cells. In a number of prisons, the organisation has even helped inmates create Buddhist gardens where they can go to meditate.

> 4 What Buddhist ideas might it be helpful for a prisoner to think about? Why?

B Buddhist zen garden at HMP Erlestoke.

> 5 Do you think it is right that religions are taught in prisons? List the benefits and disadvantages.

In 2003, Ajahn Khemadhammo was awarded an OBE for his services to prisoners. In December of 2004 he was made a 'Chao Khun' or 'Noble Lord' at the Grand Palace in Bangkok on the King of Thailand's birthday with the title Chao Khun Bhavanavitayt. This is a little bit like being made a bishop by the Queen.

Apart from some funding from NOMS for its role as the Buddhist Religious Consultative Service, Angulimala is funded entirely by charitable donations.

To find out more about Ajahn Khemadhammo and his work with Angulimala, visit the websites. See www.nelsonthornes.com/religionandbeliefs.

Assessment for Unit 3

Through the ages, Buddhism has been a religion with two faces: an inward-facing one that focuses on understanding the truth about the 'self'; and an outward-facing one that focuses on developing compassion towards others. However, as time has passed, it has become increasingly obvious that just having compassionate thoughts about others is not enough; it is necessary to put those thoughts into action. As the world has developed and 'shrunk', Buddhists have found themselves becoming involved in all sorts of social issues and applying Buddhist principles to them. In some ways then, the face of Buddhism in the twenty-first century has changed from that of the meditator and philosopher to that of a meditator and social activist.

These questions test different sets of skills in RE. Which skills do you need to work on? Choose the level you need and work through the tasks set.

Level 3

- Explain why lay Buddhists or 'upasakas' give money and food to bhikkhus.
- Buddhists have different views on animal experimentation. Say what they are and what the reasons for those different views are.
- You have won a competition to go big game hunting in Africa. Either:
  a) write a letter explaining why you cannot accept the prize, or
  b) write a letter to a Buddhist friend telling him why you have decided to go.

Level 4

- You are a Buddhist living in a country that is at war and you have just been called up to join the army. Script the conversation between yourself and a friend, telling him why you do not want to go to war.
- Explain the reasons why you would fight in a war and the reasons why you would not.
- Explain why some Buddhists are vegetarians and others are not.

Level 5

- Some present-day, 'engaged Buddhists' are actively involved in protecting the environment, while other Buddhists think such issues are not so important. Give some reasons for these *two* different views.
- Even though problems like destruction of the environment are relatively new, it is possible to find some early advice on 'Buddhist environmentalism'. What was that advice and why did Buddhists follow it?
- Do you think issues like the environment are really important? Why/why not?

Level 6

- The Monkey King's last words were: 'If my death shows you that a true king rules by love and not by the sword, then I can die without regret'. What did he mean by this? Do you agree with him? Give reasons for your answer.
- Explain why Buddhist teachings on patience and non-aggression might be difficult to practice in today's world.
- How do you think other people might see someone who decided to put those teachings into practice, no matter what? What effect might that person have on other people?

Glossary

There are two main languages in Buddhism: Sanskrit (Skrt) and Pali (P). Sanskrit is the language of Mahayana Buddhism, and Pali the language of Theravada or 'Hinayana' Buddhism.

Abhidhamma   (P) (Skrt *Abhidharma*) 'Further teachings.' Based on the teachings contained in the Suttas, the Abhidhamma is a systematic listing of the different parts of human experience.

Anatta   (P) 'Not self.' The Buddhist belief that no real 'self' can be found within the mind or body.

Anicca   (P) Impermanence: the idea that everything changes all the time.

Arhat   (Skrt) (P *Arahant*) A being who has achieved the personal liberation of Nirvana.

Bhikkhu   (P) A Buddhist monk.

Big Bang   The theory that the universe began with a giant explosion.

Bodhisattva   (Skrt) 'Enlightened being.' A follower of the Mahayana path who wishes to achieve enlightenment in order to free all beings from suffering.

Buddha   'The awakened one', 'Enlightened one'. A being who has escaped the cycle of birth and death and has fully developed the compassion and power to help lead others out of that cycle.

Compassion   The wish for others to be free from suffering.

Craving   Wanting something.

Deforestation   The destruction of forests by cutting and burning.

Desire   Wanting something based on the belief that it will bring real lasting happiness.

Dharma   (Skrt) (P *Dhamma*) 'Truth'; Buddhist teachings.

Dukkha   (P) Suffering.

Engaged Buddhist   A Buddhist who 'engages' in social actions for the benefit of others.

Enlightenment   A state of perfect wisdom, compassion and power. The final goal of Mahayana Buddhism.

Evolution   The theory that life on earth gradually developed over a long time.

Five Precepts   The basic moral code of all Buddhists not to kill; steal; lie; commit sexual misconduct; become intoxicated.

Four Noble Truths   Existence is suffering; suffering has a cause; suffering can be brought to an end; this can be achieved by following the path to the end of suffering (that is, the Noble Eightfold Path).

Guru   A spiritual master.

Hinayana   'Lesser vehicle.' The form of Buddhism that focuses on a person achieving personal liberation or 'nirvana'.

Ignorance   In Theravada Buddhism, the belief that a 'self' can be found within the mind and body. In Mahayana Buddhism, the belief that neither the person nor any other object has 'self' nature.

Insight meditation   Meditation on the true nature of reality.

Karma   (Skrt) (P *Kamma*) 'Action', the law of cause and effect; the belief that all actions have consequences.

Lama   A Tibetan name for a spiritual teacher.

Lineage   A line of teachers and students, gurus and disciples, stretching back over time to enlightened masters. Here, teachings and understanding are passed down in an unbroken line, from one generation to the next.

Love   The wish for others to be happy.

Mahayana   (Skrt) 'Great Vehicle.' The form of Buddhism that focuses on achieving enlightenment for the sake of all beings.

Meditation   Thinking about something very deeply in silence and with deep concentration.

Middle way   A way of life that runs between the two extremes of having everything you want and giving everything up. In Buddhism, this usually refers to the Noble Eightfold Path.

Multiverse   An infinite set of universes.

Nirvana   (Skrt) (P *Nibbana*) 'Extinction.' The state of individual liberation from the cycle of birth and death. NB *Not* the same as enlightenment.

Noble Eightfold Path   The main practice of Theravadin, 'Hinayana' Buddhists. The eight parts of the path are: Right understanding; Right intention; Right speech; Right action; Right livelihood; Right effort; Right mindfulness; and Right concentration.

Non-sentient   Without consciousness.

Realm   A place or state of rebirth.

Rebirth   To be born into different realms.

Reforestation   The replanting of areas of land with trees and vegetation.

Refuge   A place, thing or person one visits to escape suffering.

Samsara   The cycle of uncontrolled birth, death and rebirth.

Sangha   The community of all Buddhists. In Theravadin countries, the community of monks.

Scriptures   The written word of the Buddha and other enlightened beings.

Sentient   Possessing consciousness.

Social code   A set of rules that members of society live by.

Source of authority   Something you turn to when you need information you believe you can trust absolutely.

Sutta   (P) (Skrt *Sutra*) The written teachings of the Buddha.

Ten negative actions   Killing; stealing; sexual misconduct; harsh speech; lying; slander; idle gossip; covetousness; harmful thoughts; holding wrong views.

Theravada   'Tradition of the Elders.' The 'Hinayana' Buddhism of Thailand, Sri Lanka, Burma, Cambodia.

Three Jewels of Refuge   Buddha, Dharma, Sangha.

Three Universal Truths   Impermanence (Anicca), Selflessness (Anatta), Suffering (Dukkha).

Tipitaka   (P) (Skrt *Tripitaka*) 'The Three Baskets': Sutta, Vinaya, Abhidhamma.

Tsunami   Tidal wave caused by the movement of the earth's crust in an earthquake or volcano.

Upasaka   (P) (Skrt *Upasika*) Layman/layperson.

Vegetarian   Someone who does not eat meat.

Vinaya   The rules of Buddhist life.

Visual aid   An image or picture used to help in teaching.

Index